Look what's in the

# PYRAMID
# ENERGY
# HANDBOOK

- Straightforward answers to the questions most often asked of Dr. Serge V. King at his lectures and classes.
- Detailed instructions on how to set up experiments in a scientific manner and how to verify results.
- Information on experiments in the field upon which to develop your own investigations.
- Methods and formulas for building your own pyramids inexpensively and accurately.
- Suggestions on the best materials to use for constructing your own pyramids and where to find them.
- Sources for readymade pyramids.
- Drawings and photographs to clarify the principles and projects.
- A complete bibliography of books about pyramids so that you can follow up any aspect of special interest to you.

# PYRAMID ENERGY HANDBOOK

by
Serge V. King, Ph.D.

**WARNER BOOKS**

A Warner Communications Company

WARNER BOOKS EDITION

Copyright © 1977 by Serge V. King, Ph.D.
All rights reserved

ISBN 0-446-92029-0

Cover design by Gene Light

Cover photograph by The New Studio

Warner Books, Inc., 75 Rockefeller Plaza, New York, N.Y. 10019

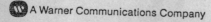 A Warner Communications Company

*Printed in the United States of America*

Not associated with Warner Press, Inc. of Anderson, Indiana

First Printing: January, 1977

Reissued: March, 1979

10  9  8  7  6  5

# Table of Contents

# PYRAMID
# ENERGY
# HANDBOOK

# Chapter 1

# WHAT IS A PYRAMID?

Maybe you already know a lot about pyramid energy and maybe you don't. Those of us who have been researching in this field for years tend to take it for granted that the rest of the world knows what we're doing. But several times recently I have mentioned pyramid energy to people and they had either heard a vague reference somewhere or else they thought I was talking about a sales system. So in this book I am not going to take anything for granted. I'm going to speak directly to you, the reader, and I'm going to introduce you to the exciting world of pyramid energy in such a way that you can easily and inexpensively begin to reap some of its many benefits. For a pyramid does work, free of charge once it's constructed. It can save you time and money, and bring you peace of mind and body. I personally think its rediscovery is the greatest thing that's happened to humanity in this century.

During classes and lectures on the pyramid and its properties I have been asked a great many stimulating and pertinent questions from the audience. They provide the basis for the question-and-answer format used throughout most of the book. Are you ready? Then let's head for adventure!

*Just before we head for adventure,*
*what exactly is a pyramid?*

A pyramid is, first of all, a geometrical form. (See Fig. 1.) It has a square base and four

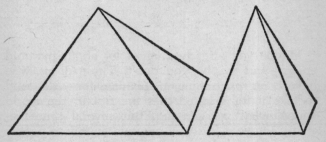

**Figure 1**

triangle-shaped sides that meet at a point at the top, called the apex or vertex. As you can see from the diagram, pyramids vary greatly in appearance according to the proportions between the length of the base and the height. However, in the field of pyramid energy, most people are working with models that duplicate more or less the proportions of the Great Pyramid of Egypt. In general terms, this is a pyramid in which the edges of the sides are slightly shorter than the edges of the base.

(See Fig. 2.) The specific proportions will be given in the chapter on building your own pyramid.

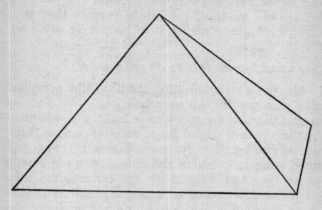

**Figure 2**

### *What's so special about the proportions of the Great Pyramid?*

The Great Pyramid was designed in a very special manner by someone who was a whiz in mathematics, physics, geology, and astronomy, to name a few of the sciences represented in that particular structure. The proportions and the resulting angles of the Great Pyramid make it an effective instrument for land surveying, determining latitudes and longitudes, setting up a worldwide system of measures, observing the stars as accurately as with a telescope, and doing such far-out mathematical tricks as squaring the circle and cubing the sphere. Actually, there are whole books on what can be done with the proportions of the Great Pyramid. Now, there are some arche-

ologists who will tell you that this was all acci-
dental. While it is true that we don't know whether
the Great Pyramid was used for all the things it
is capable of, it seems pretty certain that it is
capable of too much for it to be merely accident.

## But what has all this to do with energy?

Ah, there's the exciting part! While everyone
else was arguing about when and why and by
whom the Great Pyramid was built, a Frenchman
by the name of André Bovis noted a curious thing
while visiting the pyramid: Some garbage and
dead animals in one of the rooms were not smelly
as he expected them to be. On examination they
gave the appearance of being mummified. Something inspired him to build an exact model of the
Great Pyramid when he got back to France and
experiment with it by placing raw meats of various
kinds within to see what would happen. What
happened was that the meat did not decay as
might have been expected. Instead, it seemed to
dehydrate, or mummify, without the odor of putre-
faction. This was an astounding discovery, and
Bovis tried to present it to scientific circles for
study. Unfortunately, he was also involved in
some research which we would now call parapsychological and which his contemporaries considered quite unscientific, so they refused to even
consider what he had found. But as far as we know
in modern times, André Bovis was the first to
discover that some kind of actual energy is oper-
ating within the pyramid form. For his scale
models and all those since still perform in the
same way.

## So the exact proportions are critical?

Oh, now, I didn't say that. In fact, this is one of the myths that has grown up in the pyramid energy field already and needs to be discarded. I'd like to point out that many of the scale models in use today are more accurately proportioned than the original. Not all the base edges of the Great Pyramid are even equal, for instance. The idea that every model *must* be built to *exact* proportions or it will not work is totally false. That kind of thinking not only produces unnecessary anxiety in the minds of do-it-yourselfers, but it inhibits research. In reality, quite a bit of tolerance or variation in proportion is possible before the energy effects are greatly diminished. I think it's safe to say that a pyramid in which all the edges are of equal length will work just as well as one based on the proportions of the Great Pyramid.

## Then why all the emphasis on proportions?

The proportions of the Great Pyramid are esthetically pleasing to the eye, for one thing. For another, there are psychological associations with Egypt that are desirable for some people. Finally, the proportions of the Great Pyramid contain mathematical information that may lead to other information and other discoveries. I think the Great Pyramid was built the way it was primarily as a means of passing on knowledge. The energy could have been produced with other proportions, but not the knowledge.

*I've heard that the Great Pyramid
was just a tomb for a Pharaoh.*

If there's anything the Great Pyramid was *not*,
it was a Pharaoh's tomb. This is the claim of traditional archeologists who have nothing to base it
on except what they think it should be. You see,
in spite of the movies we've seen, no body or
mummy has ever been found in any pyramid except perhaps a couple of very small ones built
thousands of years after the Great Pyramid was
supposed to have been built. (If any of you archeologists out there can correct me, I will back down
gracefully. Please accept this as a challenge.) Any
idea you hear today about who built the Great
Pyramid and why is only based on guesswork or
intuition. The Egyptians, who were meticulous
recorders, have left no written records about the
Great Pyramid. Even the date of construction
is in question. It is usually given as 3500 B.C.,
but this is based on the flimsiest of evidence. If
you read much about pyramids you will often
hear the name Cheops given to the Great Pyramid.
This is the name of the Pharaoh who ruled during
the above date. It does not prove that he is the
one who had it built. As far as pyramid research
goes, it really doesn't matter very much. What
matters is the energy and how we can use it.

*But do you think the ancient
Egyptians knew about the energy?*

Personally, I do. First, there are mathematical
concepts within the proportions of the Great
Pyramid that point out the location of highest

energy concentration (math nuts are referred to my previous book, *Mana Physics*, for an explanation of *phi* and its relation to the energy focal point). Second, the construction of critical rooms in association with areas of highest energy concentration seems to indicate this. Third, there are the mummies, regardless of where they were buried. One of the effects of the energy is to mummify dead flesh, and the ancient Egyptian system of mummification is still unknown. Most Egyptologists think they had a special kind of embalming fluid. I think they treated the corpses in a pyramid before they buried them.

## Could the energy have been used to build the pyramid?

This is a fun area for speculation. The Great Pyramid could have been built in a dozen different ways without resorting to a special kind of energy. On the other hand, there are hints in recent research that the energy in question may have antigravitational effects. If so, and if the Egyptians (or whoever—we don't even know for sure who built it) knew a practical way to focus the energy for this use, they would have been silly not to use it. But at this point we have no way of proving or disproving it.

## What happened after Bovis was rejected by the scientists?

Things progressed very slowly. It was in the thirties that Bovis made his discovery. Two Americans, Verne Cameron and Ralph Bergstresser, did pyramid research in the forties, but received no better treatment than Bovis did. Also in the forties Karl Drbal, a Czechoslovakian, discovered the fact that a pyramid will sharpen razor blades (that's right!), but it took him ten years of struggle to get a patent. Finally, Sheila Ostrander and Lynn Schroeder published a book called *Psychic Discoveries Behind The Iron Curtain* in which they devoted a chapter to pyramid research in Czechoslovakia and started a mini-boom in pyramid interest in the United States. Since then a lot of "underground" research has been going on, most of which is being done in garages and basements and very little of which is being published as yet. More pyramids are being built than information is being printed about what they do. Pyramid interest is quickly building up a fad.

*Are pyramids becoming
commercially available, then?*

They certainly are. At the end of this book is a list of suppliers. The pyramids available vary greatly in cost, size, and construction. They come in cardboard, aluminum, steel, copper, wood, lucite, styrene, and even stone. Some are only three inches high, while others being planned rival the original. Houses, hotels, and rooms are being built in pyramid form, and pyramids are being joined together in various ways for supposedly better effects.

*Does it matter what
material the pyramid is made from?*

In general, no. That is, you will get basically the same effects no matter what material you use.

But many people report that the energy in pyramids of certain materials feels different to them than when other materials are used. Some prefer copper and say that it is "stronger" than other materials. Others like wood because it is "softer." Naturally, these are very subjective terms.

## How do you measure the energy?

That's a good question that deserves a better answer than anyone is able to give just yet. One of the problems with pyramid energy is that it doesn't respond to any ordinary devices for measuring electricity or magnetism. Sometimes it acts like electricity, sometimes like magnetism, and sometimes it even acts like light, but it isn't any of these. That's why measurement is such a problem. At the present time, to my knowledge, and notwithstanding certain vague claims that have been made, there are five ways to measure the pyramid energy. Unfortunately, none of these is precise enough to suit a scientific laboratory.

## I don't have a scientific laboratory, so let's have them.

Well, the most objective kind of measurement is by observing the effects. For instance, one kind or size of pyramid might dehydrate or sharpen a blade faster than another. That gives you a kind of relative measurement. A surprisingly objective measurement technique involves a lightweight pendulum. The best thing I have found for this is a plastic container such as you find in gumball machines. You take off the cap, poke a hole through it with a needle followed by the end of a

length of thread, tie a button on the end of the
thread, and replace the cap on the container. The
thread should be ten to twelve inches long. (See
Fig. 3.) Now you take this pendulum, holding it

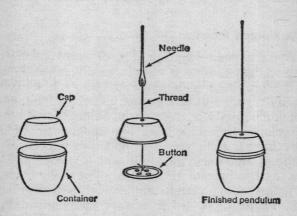

Figure 3

by the free end, and bring it slowly near the side
of the pyramid or over the tip. The effect you are
going to notice will be very slight, so you have to
pay close attention. As you come closer to the
pyramid, you will feel a faint resistance against
the pendulum, as if it were moving against
"thicker air." This is not just your imagination,
though some people may be able to feel it more
easily than others. To prove how objective it is,
notice how the pendulum goes "out of plumb" or
away from the vertical as you meet the resistance
of the pyramid energy field. You can even have
a friend watch from the side to verify this effect.

With pyramids of different intensity, you will notice a difference in the resistance of the field and in the distance from the pyramid that you first feel it. These two methods of measurement can be used by anybody.

### And the others?

Now we have to get very subjective. *Most* people can feel something when they place a hand inside or above a pyramid. The usual sensations are warmth, a cool breeze, pressure, or tingling. The sensations experienced vary from person to person, and even within the same person at various times. This makes it hard to do any accurate measurement, but it does indicate that energy is present. Once you get to know your own reactions pretty well, you will be able to make a rough estimate of energy differences between pyramids. You should know, however, that there are some people who will not feel a thing. If you happen to be one, don't let it bug you. Your sensitivity will increase the longer you work with pyramids. Until then you'll just have to use another method. The next method requires some skill at "dowsing" or radiesthesia, the same ability that enables certain people to find water with a forked stick. If you don't believe in it, that's okay. Try something else. If you happen to know, as I do, that it can be done, and you know how to do it, you can use the pendulum described above or your favorite dow instrument. A good dowser can get ver readings. This isn't a book on dow I can't explain the process h a good explanation of i the last method.

can see the energy. That may sound wild, but such people do exist. We were not all born with a standard range of sensory perception. Some of us have, among other things, a broader spectrum of vision than the rest. As an aside, most people can be trained to extend the spectrum they have, but that is the subject of another book. At any rate, if you can find someone who can see the energy radiating from a pyramid, you have an edge on most other researchers.

*I've heard something about the*
*"King's Chamber." What does that mean?*

The King's Chamber refers to a focal point of energy approximately one-third of the distance from the base to the apex in the center of the pyramid. The name comes from a room in the Great Pyramid so named because it had a flat roof like the burial chambers the Arabs used for men. You see, it was the Arabs who first broke into the Great Pyramid. They also found another room with a peaked roof and called it the Queen's Chamber because that's the kind of room they buried their women in. No bodies or treasure were found in either room. (See Fig. 4 for a layout of the rooms.) Both the King's Chamber and the Queen's Chamber are close to where the focal point should be in the Great Pyramid, though neither one is exactly located there. The King's Chamber is now the nickname for the focal point in pyramid models.

*Is the energy only at the focal point?*

at all. That's only the point of greatest con-

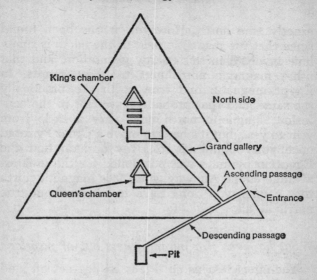

**Figure 4**

centration. There is energy all around the inside, around the outside, and projecting off the tip and the base corners. These facts were discovered by dowsers and have since been utilized to make the pyramid more versatile. You will find out in what ways later on.

## Does it matter which way the pyramid faces?

Yes! That is very important. The energy field associated with a pyramid seems to be strongest when *one side* of the pyramid is facing magnetic north. Magnetic north is where the needle of a compass points. It is not the same thing as true north. In the early days of pyramid experimentation it was thought that the pyramid should face true north because the Great Pyramid faces almost exactly true north. However, it has been found since that the magnetic field of the earth is somehow involved in this energy generation, and that using magnetic north gets the best results. In Egypt magnetic and true north are practically the same, and that probably gave rise to the confusion. Magnetic north does vary a little from year to year, but it's hard to move a Great Pyramid once you've built it. It is my opinion that the Egyptian pyramid was positioned for the greatest average effect. Anyway, since it is magnetic north that counts, you don't have to worry about true north at all.

## What happens if a pyramid gets out of position?

The effect lessens until it is 45 degrees off, and then it builds up again if the pyramid continues to turn. In other words, the least effective position is when a corner is facing magnetic north. The effect never entirely disappears; it just gets weaker.

## Where can I get a compass?

Some pyramid kits include a compass. Otherwise you can try a sporting goods store or a toy store. You don't need an expensive compass, since a little variation is tolerable. Don't forget that the Great Pyramid isn't right on, either. You can make your own compass easily enough with a bar magnet of any size. A bar magnet is just a magnet that is shaped like a bar. Tie a string or thread around the middle and let the magnet hang loose. When it finally stops spinning it will come to rest in a north/south position. You don't really have to know which is north and which is south, since one side of your pyramid will be facing each way. As a desperation measure, face one side of your pyramid to the direction in which the sun sets or rises. That will align the other two sides and you're in business. That isn't as accurate as the other ways, but it will do for most things.

### Does a pyramid have to have a base?

There are some reports that say a pyramid works better with a base made of the same material. But in my experiments I haven't found any significant difference.

### I've seen pyramids without sides. Do they work?

Astonishingly enough, they do. The first pyramid models had solid sides. Then a few people made holes in them to see how large they could be and still work. They still worked with large holes in the sides. Finally, somebody tried it with just the framework of a pyramid and it still worked, almost as well as with solid sides. The difference is really minimal. Interestingly enough, side panels without corners do not seem to work, and neither do frameworks without a connecting base frame. The advantages of a framework pyramid are that you can see your experiments in progress, you can put things in and take them out without disturbing the set-up, and you can move them around more easily. This discovery was a real breakthrough.

### Some people have pyramids hanging from the ceiling. What about that?

Another significant discovery was that the

energy from a pyramid seems to project downward, almost as if a small pyramid held off the
floor were the capstone or tip of a larger invisible
pyramid. This means that if you suspend a pyramid from the ceiling you will get the same effects
under it that you would get inside it. Although
a lot of people are doing this now, no one has yet
reported any studies showing what the energy
loss is, if any. All we know right now is that you
do get effects.

### Do larger pyramids give off more energy?

That does seem to be the case, taking into
account differences in materials.

### What is a pyramid grid?

This is a group of pyramids arranged so as to
get an accumulative effect from the energy pour-
ing out of the tips. One model has fifteen pyramids
about one inch high and is the size of a postcard.
You put things on top of the grid to be treated.
Other grids have been made of groups of framework pyramids. They do work.

### And what is a pyramid plate?

A pyramid plate usually refers to a piece of
coated aluminum sheeting that has been zapped
with about 100,000 volts of electricity to make it
temporarily produce the same effects as a pyramid.
It should not be confused with my own invention,
the Manaplate, which is a permanent "pyramid"
energy generator utilizing principles discovered
by Wilhelm Reich. The fact is, pyramids are only

one way in which this same energy can be produced.

## Why isn't the government doing any research on pyramid energy?

First of all, the government *is* sponsoring a certain amount of research on pyramid energy. An organization called Mankind Research Unlimited in Washington, D. C., received a government grant to do some basic research and its findings substantiated much of what private researchers have already said. Probably more research is going on than is publicly acknowledged. Not long ago a story was carried in major newspapers about a U.S. government-financed project in Egypt supposedly to locate a possible hidden room in the Great Pyramid. This was undertaken by positioning cosmic-ray recording apparatus around the base of the pyramid. The idea was that by correlating the differences in cosmic ray tracks a hidden room could be located. The first report out of Egypt said that, contrary to the laws of physics, the idea didn't work because the recordings were different every day. That shouldn't have happened, and there was no explanation. Of course, a later report came out denying the first report. Anyway, as I recall, the project was funded to the tune of about a million dollars. With watchdogs like Senators Church and Proxmire around, I doubt very much whether that much money would be spent just to locate a possible hidden room. I admit I'm speculating, but I think the project had more to do with investigating the energy properties of the pyramid.

### What do scientists think about pyramid energy?

The problem is that most scientists don't even think about it if they can help it. The "world of science" is a pretty tricky subculture to survive in. If you get too far away from the mainstream of thought you are either ignored or destroyed, depending on the waves you make. And for the moment, pyramid research is *way* outside the mainstream of established scientific thinking. Fortunately, there are a few very hardy and brave scientists who are looking into it in a serious way—on their own time, naturally, and with a great deal of caution, but they are going ahead. Just a few days before this page was written I was told of research going on in a West Coast university which is confirming the claims of the better private researchers and which is uncovering some important magnetic effects as well. I was told that the results are "publishable" and that an outlet is now being sought. In the scientific subculture, getting your results published is one of the main difficulties, especially if dearly held tenets are questioned. Holding hope for the future is the fact that more and more high school science classes and science fairs are encouraging or accepting pyramid energy projects by the students.

### You mentioned a few things that pyramids are supposed to do. What else?

I'll give you a list here, in no particular order, of the most common claims being made. We'll discuss them in detail in later chapters.

—sharpening of razor blades and cutlery

—mellowing coffee, tea, and tobacco
—making tap water taste like spring water
—stimulation of plant growth
—speeding up of seed germination time
—preservation of food
—enhancement of natural flavors
—ripening of fruits and vegetables
—retardation of algae growth and inhibition of bacterial growth
—improvement of TV and radio reception
—recharging of batteries
—increased awareness and profound relaxation
—stimulation of the healing process and easement of pain
—increased vitality and virility
—retardation and removal of tarnish

## It sounds like a snake-oil salesman's cure-all. How can it do all that?

The fact that pyramid energy does so many different things is one of the major problems in convincing people that it works, and in trying to figure out how it does work. In the next chapter we are going to look at some theories about how pyramid energy operates. If you like that kind of speculation, you should enjoy that chapter and perhaps come up with some ideas of your own.

If, however, you are eager to get down to practical application, you can skip Chapter 2 and head right into Chapter 3, where we will tell you exactly how to start experimenting by yourself.

# Chapter 2

# HOW DOES IT WORK?

It is inevitable. Every time I give a talk on pyramid energy, someone will look me straight in the eye and ask, "How does it work?" No matter that we still do not understand the workings of electricity, magnetism, gravity, light, the human body, and a host of other things in the world. There seems to be an essential human need to ask the question and to receive an answer that fits somewhere into the questioner's framework of knowledge. In the old days it was easy. You could say, "the gods" or "God" makes it happen. Today the answers have to be more technical or people get uncomfortable. It doesn't matter how outlandish they are, as long as they sound good. Of course, to the more wide-awake mind the answer must also sound reasonable, but most of the time a comfortable answer is all that is required.

An answer to the question of how a particular type of energy works is called a theory, which means (at best) an educated guess. You should understand that we do not have answers to how electricity, magnetism, etc., work, but only guesses, that is, theories. The best kind of theory is one that explains practically all the phenomena associated with the subject under question, and which can be used to predict future phenomena. When a theory gets that good, it is usually accepted as fact—at least, until some phenomenon comes along that it doesn't explain. Then you need a new theory.

I said that theories could be outlandish as long as they sound good. Even the most serious scientists fall into this trap, especially when a new phenomenon comes along that upsets their old theories. Not long ago I heard a scientist give his theory of some magnetic happenings on the sun. First he talked about magnetic lines of force, which he said were only imaginary but convenient concepts. Then he demonstrated how these imaginary lines flowed around the sun. Finally, he said that the new phenomenon he was explaining worked by means of imaginary rings spinning along the imaginary lines of force and changing from one imaginary line to another. At the end he seriously believed that he had given a clear explanation. If nothing else, it was a good use of imagination.

Another style of scientific theory was presented at a conference on exobiology, the study of life on places other than the earth (totally excluding UFO considerations). The phenomenon to be explained was the presence of biological forms in certain meteorites. One scientist of considerable standing got up and proposed the theory that a long time ago a huge meteorite had crashed on the earth, causing bits of earth to splash up and land on the moon; then, later on, a meteorite had crashed on the moon, causing those same bits to fall back to earth. What is so sad is that the theory was proposed and listened to in all seriousness.

The first theory used the technique of constructing an imaginary set of circumstances and explaining phenomena in terms of those circumstances. Starting with a false or unprovable assumption, it is possible to prove or explain anything you like. The second type of theory stuck with known facts, but strung them together in an absurd way and with complete disregard for other known facts. For example, biological forms are found in some meteorites, and meteorites do strike both the earth and the moon, but a meteorite striking the earth would not be able to transfer enough of its kinetic energy to enable struck particles to attain the 7 miles per second velocity necessary to break them free of the earth's gravitational field.

If you haven't already guessed, what I'm trying to do is to make you wary of any theories proposed to explain pyramid energy, especially at this stage of research. In other words, don't accept them just because they sound good, or just because they happen to fit your present set of beliefs. Try to keep two questions in mind: Does the theory explain all known phenomena, and can it be used to predict future phenomena? At present, no theory on pyramid energy meets both these criteria very well. What we are trying to do is to find one that comes closest.

With this *caveat* out of the way, I will now

present some of the more current theories that you will run across. To save some people embarrassment, I will not mention the names of the originators except in my own case. And I hereby give you permission to laugh at me all you like.

## The Ether Vortex Theory

According to this theory, there is a thing called the "ether," a subatomic or proto-atomic fluid permeating and connecting everything in the physical universe. Gravity is supposed to be a function of pressure of the ether, and electromagnetic forces are the function of vortices (whirlpools or eddies) in the etheric fluid. The pyramid shape is supposed to cause such an electromagnetic vortex, and this is supposed to explain the associated phenomena. This is tantamount to saying that pyramid energy phenomena are caused by electromagnetism. If so, it means that we know even less about electromagnetism than we thought we did, which is certainly possible. As you will find out in a later chapter, pyramid energy definitely does have electromagnetic effects, although no measurements of electromagnetism as we know it have yet been made in regard to the pyramid, to my knowledge. Strangely enough, a number of pyramid energy effects also occur in the presence of electrical devices and magnets, lending credibility to the theory. However, other effects apparently occur in the absence of electromagnetism in any known form, thus detracting from the theory. At any rate, the theory offers only a very generalized explanation without saying why the pyramid shape should be different from a cube in its effects, and how the energy produces the effects it does. All in all, it is not very satisfactory.

## Microwave Resonance

This theory has the advantage of sounding very scientific and of having the endorsement of Karl Drbal, the Czech radio technician who discovered the razor-blade sharpening or regeneration effect. The theoretical explanation of microwave resonance was accepted by the Czechoslovakian patent board when Drbal got his patent on the pyramid razor-blade sharpener. I should point out that Drbal discovered, as I did, that the pyramid form is not the only geometric form which can produce the energy effects, and that the Great Pyramid proportions are not the only effective ones. As to the theory, Drbal postulated that a pyramid made of dielectric (that is, nonmetallic) material would allow the penetration of microwaves from electric, magnetic, electromagnetic, gravitic, corpuscular, and perhaps other not yet defined sources. Because there would only be a partial repenetration outward through the dielectric material, the remaining microwaves would set up a process of resonant excitation within the pyramid cavity. This process is thought to produce an acceleration in the regeneration of the crystalitic structure of the edge of the blade. You see, a razor blade has a "live" crystalline edge. That means that if you just leave the blade alone after using it it will regenerate itself to a considerable extent in a little less than a month. The pyramid accelerates this process so that it takes place within 24 hours. Another action of the microwave resonance is to drive out the water molecules from the edge of the blade into the open air. According to Drbal, water acting on steel can reduce its firmness by as much as 22 percent. This resonant action on water molecules also is supposed to account for the dehydration or mummification process on organic matter. Studies of electromagnetic dehydration confirm that this is what happens. The microwave action also has a sterilization effect. In other words, it can kill microorganisms which cause decay, thus producing some of the other effects of the pyramid on living and dead organic matter. Since microwave action is supposed to be involved, Drbal feels that pyramids, to be effective, must be made of nonmetallic materials because microwaves would be screened out by metals. For the same reason he feels it should not be used on or near electromagnetic devices or metal walls.

I have mentioned Drbal's name not only because he deserves credit for the important research he has done, but because of his true scientific spirit. A true scientist is always ready to admit he might have been wrong when new knowledge contradicts a hypothesis he has held. Drbal has clearly stated that microwave resonance might not be involved and that his theory could be mistaken. I'm glad to hear that because recent discoveries do not uphold the microwave theory. For one thing, it has been found that metal pyramids work just as well as nonmetal ones. For another thing, pyramid frameworks will also do the job, which seems to dispose of the idea of resonant excitation. Furthermore, my own experiments indicate that metallic walls do not inhibit the action of the pyramid and that electromagnetic devices frequently enhance or amplify the pyramid effect, rather than reduce it. So while the microwave resonance theory may explain some effects, it has done a poor job of predicting other effects.

## Magnetic Theory

There is no doubt that magnetism is intimately involved with pyramid energy. There is a theory, however, that magnetism is the only thing involved. There is still a lot about magnetism that we do not know, and a lot which is known but not yet fully accepted. It is known, for instance, that the pyramid works best when aligned with one side facing magnetic north. At that point the pyramid energy seems to be most highly concentrated. As the pyramid is moved out of alignment, the effects lessen until the least effects are obtained when a corner is facing magnetic north. That does not mean the effects totally disappear, they just aren't as strong. In experimenting with a three-sided pyramid—a tetrahedron—I was surprised to find that it did not seem to be necessary to align it in order to get the effects, which are the same as in a regular pyramid. However, this may be explained by the fact that an equilateral three-sided pyramid can never be more than 20 to 25 degrees off magnetic north (or south; it makes no difference). So it can never be as much out of alignment as a true pyramid. (See Fig. 5.)

The magnetic theory is supported by evidence which shows magnetic readings on a gauss meter even within cardboard pyramids, readings which increase as the pyramid is oriented toward north. The readings were greater on metal-frame pyramids, but this is not as natural as it might sound, for by rights the metal frame should have shielded or absorbed magnetic energies from within the

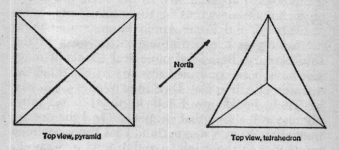

Top view, pyramid                              Top view, tetrahedron

**Figure 5**

framework. The fact that it didn't is quite significant. Apparently, vertical orientation is only one
necessity. Bill Kerrell and Kathy Goggin, who
reported the above experiment, in their book The
Guide to Pyramid Energy also found that magnetic energies decreased as the base of the pyramid
was tilted from the horizontal until little or no
effect was detectable with the pyramid completely
inverted. Supporting the above evidence is some
information I received from a researcher at a western university. His independent findings confirm
the magnetic effects around pyramids of all materials. My own research points out the importance
of the earth's magnetic field in the blade regeneration effect. The Manaplate, a flat plate of no particular shape, does not need to be oriented to
achieve any of the pyramid energy effects, *but* the
best sharpening effect is obtained when the *blade*
is oriented with its long axis north and south.

Magnetism has long been thought to have special properties above and beyond its present technological applications. In 200 B.C., the Greek physician Galen wrote of the healing properties of magnets, and Franz Anton Mesmer used them extensively at the beginning of his work in the 18th century. Beneficial biological effects of magnets have been confirmed recently by the excellent research of Albert Roy Davis and Walter C. Rawls, Jr. Their books are listed in the bibliography. My research shows that people can feel the energy emanating from a magnet and that the sensations are similar to those felt in and around a pyramid. What's more, in subjective tests run with many volunteers I have found that people are quite sensitive to the earth's magnetic field. Other researchers, as well, have also discovered that placing a magnet inside a pyramid seems to amplify the effect.

A number of findings apparently refute the magnetic theory, however. Mesmer, for instance, finally did away with magnets because he found they were unnecessary for achieving his energy effects. As for myself, I have obtained all the pyramid effects with the use of nonmagnetic materials, though the need for blade orientation remains an anomaly. Kerrel and Goggin reported that placing a strong magnetic field around a test substance did not produce the same effects as a pyramid, but in fairness it should be stated that other research indicates that weak magnetic fields paradoxically have a greater effect on biological substances than strong ones. And a grid or matrix of inverted pyramids will produce the regular pyramid energy effects.

So where do we stand on the magnetic theory?

Until it can be shown that nonmagnetic substances are really magnetic, after all, it will have to be considered as insufficient to explain all the effects produced.

## Radiation Theory

This theory, I maintain, supported by much scientific evidence, that everything radiates electromagnetic energy through the oscillation of atoms or molecular systems. Energy is transferred from one substance to another when the second substance resonates or vibrates in harmony with the radiation of the first substance. Simple examples of this are seen when a singer reaches a note that causes a glass to break, when a tuning fork causes a nearby stringed instrument to hum, or when a static electric generator causes a fluorescent bulb to light at a distance. With regard to pyramids, the radiation theory holds that the radiant energy of the pyramid structure combines at the angles or corners to form beams extending both inward and outward from the pyramid. Where they meet inside the pyramid is the well-known focal point, or King's Chamber. As the process continues, the air inside the pyramid begins to vibrate in harmony with the beams until the whole interior atmosphere is saturated, thus giving rise to the effects. As it happens, beams of energy have been detected off the corners and the apex, and it is known that the effects of a pyramid continue even below it.

The bothersome thing about this theory is that it should predict a strong energy field within a cube to produce the same effects as a pyramid. Yet, many experiments show that a cube does not prevent decay of organic material, for example, in the same way as a pyramid does. On the other hand, the scientist Wilhelm Reich did find pyramid energy-type effects inside a metal tube, and even more so when layers of organic material were added to the metal. But when such a cube is taken apart, energy still seems to radiate from the flat plates, and this seems to contradict the beam theory. One cannot say that the plates were saturated by the beams, because such layered plates work even if they have never been made into a cube. Finally, we have constructed pyramids joined by plastic tubing, which gives rounded corners, and still we get the same effects. Clearly, radiation/beam theory leaves something to be desired.

## The Cosmic Lens Theory

This one is easily disposed of. It states that the special nature of the pyramid shape causes it to act as a lens to concentrate cosmic energy streaming to the earth from outer space. If the pyramid shape were the only one to cause the phenomenon, this explanation might have some plausibility, but it isn't, and so it doesn't. The question here is not whether there is cosmic energy. It is whether the pyramid is a lens. Apart from the fact that very unlenslike shapes can work, we have to take into account the energy field surrounding the pyramid and beaming out of it. No, the lens idea has too many limitations.

## The Multi-Energy Theory

Since pyramid energy has effects that resemble

those of electricity, magnetism, gravity (or anti-gravity), static electricity, and apparently several unknown types, the easy way out has been taken by some theorists who simply say that the pyramid is a multi-energy generator. Well, folks, as a theory this one is a bust. A good theory is supposed to simplify things, not make them more complicated. And a multi-energy theory is virtually worthless as far as predictability goes. If anything can happen, or everything, there is no pattern for practical application. But the pyramid has a pattern, and the results are practical. In a sense, it may not be possible to argue against the multi-energy theory, but it neither explains nor predicts and is therefore unusable.

## The Prime Energy Theory

This theory predates anything we call civilization, yet it is the one I prefer. According to this idea there is a prime energy—some might call it cosmic energy—of which all other energies are effects. To use an analogy, you have a substance, water. Under certain conditions it may be ice, liquid, or steam. In like manner, the prime energy—I call it mana, following the tradition—Huna science under certain conditions may appear as electricity, magnetism, or gravity. This is why electricity can be converted into magnetism and vice versa. We know very little about gravity as yet, but there is no logical reason why, in addition to the electromagnetic spectrum, there might not also be a gravito-electric and gravito-magnetic spectrum as well. Both electricity and magnetism have their polarities, and pyramid energy exhibits polarity effects too. Gravity is thought by some to be monopolar, but I think the upward growth of plants, for instance, demonstrates the existence of what we can call an anti-gravity force. Do you realize how much anti-gravitational force it takes to lift a sequoia two hundred and fifty feet above the ground, or to push a blade of grass through a concrete sidewalk?

Another aspect of mana is what we might as well call "life force," that mysterious quality that promotes patterned growth, regeneration of cells, and sensory experience. The pyramid enhances all these effects. So much can be done with pyramid energy that it seems obvious there is a common denominator. The same specific effect, such as mellowing coffee, can be produced by electricity, magnetism, sunlight, pyramids, Mana-plates, or your own hands. Some common thread must connect them all. This is the Law of the Elephant: If it looks like an elephant, walks like an elephant, talks like an elephant, and acts like an elephant, then it's probably an elephant. Evidence seems to point to a prime energy. While not perfect, this theory does have advantages. It explains existing effects and does allow for predictability. As an example, based on the prime energy concept I was able to predict that an orgone box, a particular type of energy device invented by Wilhelm Reich and not of pyramid shape, would be able to produce all the effects of a pyramid, including the sharpening of razor blades, and it did. This is only one of many useful predictions that have been made based on the prime energy theory. The main advantage is that it works, until and if somebody evolves a better one.

As to where the energy of a pyramid comes

from, I think the pyramid is a condenser—not a generator, but a condenser. We are living in an ocean of prime energy, an ocean which has currents such as the earth's magnetic flow. I believe the pyramid shape causes a distortion in that flow, an eddy, so to speak, where the energy becomes more condensed and thus its effects more noticeable. You know, of course, that the earth also has an electrical field flowing perpendicular to the magnetic one. This would also be distorted, or condensed, and account for some of the electrical qualities of pyramid energy. If this idea has any truth, we should be able to design specific shapes for more specific effects. In fact, this is being done in Czechoslovakia by a metallurgist named Robert Pavlita, and by an organization called Genesa headed by Dr. Derald Langham in Fallbrook, California. Pavlita's inventions are called psychotronic devices.

## The Less Theory More Practice Theory

In practically every field of human endeavor and progress, practice has preceded theory. What usually happens is that somebody discovers something and then later somebody else tries to figure out why it worked. By then the first guy is way ahead with something else. When people experience what pyramid energy does and then ask me "How does it work?" I usually make a rough quote of Edison's remark when asked by a lady how electricity worked. "Don't worry about how it works, madam," he is said to have replied, "just use it!"

# Chapter 3

# HOW TO SET UP
# EXPERIMENTS

From listening to people's responses when you tell them some of the unusual things that even a cardboard pyramid is supposed to do, you would think that we are a society without any will power or discernment. It gets worse when you get them to try something like the taste test. The most common reaction I receive from people confronted with pyramid energy for the first time is, "Well, that's just suggestion!" What they are saying is that by merely mentioning the possibility that they would taste a difference with pyramid-treated water, I caused them to experience it. Wow! I wish I really had such power. But apparently I don't because when I then suggest that they finance some research, I only get a blank stare.

It is both amazing and ironic to realize how many people have been programmed to believe that they are easily suggestible (when experience conflicts with "logic") and that so much of reality is a function of belief. For many people think that the pyramid works if you believe in it. This can be rather disheartening for the novice researcher who is eager to share his or her knowledge with others. On the other hand, there are wild claims made by certain so-called researchers that discredit the whole field of pyramid energy because they are so easily refuted by simple experiments. In those cases, desire, or belief, does overcome reality—for the claimants, at least.

To help ease your own mind about the energy, to aid you in overcoming the healthy skepticism of friends and relatives, and to assist you in determining what pyramids can and cannot do, I am going to use the question-and-answer format to explain how to set up experiments in a scientific manner. This will give your findings more credibility, even though the National Academy of Science may not accept your results as proof of anything. The point is that by using an organized method in your research you will eliminate much of the erroneous reporting that is due to overenthusiasm or carelessness.

## *Okay, what's the first thing to do?*

Get a pyramid. That isn't as facetious as it sounds, honest. Before you begin, you must have in mind the kind of experiment you want to perform. Remember, you have your choice among pyramids of different shapes, materials, and construction (frameworks as opposed to solid sides, for example). Probably, though, you will want to begin with something small and simple. For beginning research I would recommend a cardboard pyramid 6 inches high. You can do an awful lot with that before your interest takes you into fancier, larger, and/or more expensive models.

### Then what?

Get a notebook. A spiral-bound notebook with 8½" by 11" pages is a good choice, but you might prefer a loose leaf so you can take out pages and photocopy them. This book will contain your research results. The better organized it is, the easier it will be for you to duplicate, modify, and refer back to your experiments.

At the top of the first page, put the date and the number of your first experiment. It is a good idea to number all your experiments, the easiest way being to start with "1" and head toward infinity. But if you think you will be experimenting with several kinds of pyramids, you might want to establish a simple kind of code to make reference easier. For instance, experiments with your 6-inch cardboard pyramid could be numbered CP6/1, CP6/2, CP6/3, etc. and those with a 12-inch-high aluminum frame, AF12/1, AF12/2, and so on.

Next, write down the word "Objective," and after it put down the reason you are conducting this experiment. Perhaps it is to see whether the pyramid can really sharpen razor blades or preserve fruit. Or you might be testing for the effects of turning the pyramid away from magnetic north. Whatever it is, state it clearly in this section so that you don't forget what it is you are trying to find out.

Title the following section "Materials," and list

here everything you are using for the experiment, being as specific as possible. A typical list might be "one 6-inch cardboard Cheops model pyramid; one Gillette blue blade; one plastic 2-inch stand." You will also want to list any materials you are using for comparison, such as a second blade. If you are testing liquids for taste, list the source (tap water, Yuban, Johnnie Walker) and make a notation of the temperature. For most purposes, a simple hot, warm, cool, or cold will do. This is important because temperature does affect taste.

The next section should be titled "Procedure." This is where you will describe how you are going to carry out the experiment. As an example, you could say that after shaving you are going to place a razor blade inside the pyramid on top of the stand with the long axis north and south, that you are going to leave it there for 24 hours before testing it on your beard again, and that you are going to keep up this experiment for a period of 3 weeks. It is very important that this section be well detailed, because here is where you can get ideas for modifying future experiments and perhaps find out what you did wrong if the experiment didn't seem to work.

I would suggest another section, either before or after the previous one, titled "Environment." Pyramids are well known to be cantankerous. Sometimes they don't work even when you think you've done everything right. Karl Drbal wrote that the "last twenty-five years have been for me a long experimental sequence, with each shaving itself an experimental experience which has sometimes informed me, by unexpected changes in the sharpness of the blade, of some meteorological or cosmic disturbances . . . often after a day when

I received a poor shave I was surprised the next day by receiving, from the same blade, an excellent shave." This experience is duplicated in my early research notes before I was aware of the details of Drbal's work. So, under "Environment" note weather conditions, time of day, and, if you can, the position of the moon and whether sunspots are active. In addition, make a note of where the experiment is being conducted, on what kind of surface, and whether it is close to electrical devices. There is a lot of controversy about the effect of electrical devices on pyramids. Maybe your research will help establish some facts.

"Results" is the title of the next section. Now you have a place to record what happens during your experiment. Make this part as objective as possible. Just note results as they appear to you. Make no judgments and draw no conclusions, as yet. If your experiment is ongoing, note the results by date and/or time.

Finally, you can have a section called "Conclusions." These are your conclusions based on the results of your experiment. You might decide that "the pyramid really does sharpen blades," or "the taste test was inconclusive, will have to try at a different temperature next time." In other words, it is a summary of your ideas, thoughts, criticisms, and recommendations about the experiment. This section will become a rich source of future experimental ideas.

There is no telling how much space each experimental write-up will take. It depends a lot on how much detail you like to put down, and how involved or time-consuming the experiment is. In some cases my notebook has three experiments on a single page, while in others one experiment may take five pages or more. Two factors which play a role in determining how complicated an experiment is going to be are "controls" and "variables."

### What is a control, since you obviously want the question?

Thank you. A control is something like a second experiment that goes on at the same time as another, only the conditions are changed. For example, let's say you are testing the possible change of taste in a glass of tap water after placing it under a pyramid for 5 minutes. You can taste the water first and then taste it after it has been under the pyramid, but there is the chance that you will have forgotten how it tasted in the first place. So a better way is to use a control, that is, a second glass of water drawn at the same time as the first test glass and using the same kind of container. Now, after the 5 minutes are over, you can taste the "control" glass, the one left out under ordinary conditions, and compare it to the "test" glass, the one left under the pyramid. You see, the control is the experiment in which everything is the same *except* the thing you are testing for. This helps you decide whether the thing being tested is having any effect. In testing a pyramid, another pyramid could be the control if it were disoriented by 45 degrees. That would tell you if magnetic north were having the effect it is supposed to. In using controls you have to be careful not to introduce any factors that make the experiment invalid. A glass of ice water should not be used as a control for a test glass of freshly drawn tap water, for instance. An aluminum pyra-

mid should not be tested against a cardboard one
if what you are testing for is the effect of magnetic
north and not the effect of the different materials.
The control has to be as nearly identical to the
test object as possible for a controlled experiment
to have any meaning. And controlled experiments
are much more highly regarded than uncontrolled
experiments. In some cases a control experiment
can be run at a different time than the test. You
can test a blue blade to see how many shaves you
can get from it, and then test a blue blade which
has been under a pyramid between shaves for
comparison. Then your only variables are outside
forces that might change from day to day.

### Now, may I ask, what are variables?

Experimentally speaking, a variable is anything
which changes, or which is changed. It is the
opposite of a "constant," that which does not
change. Temperature would be a variable if your
control glass of water is put outside in the winter
while your test glass is put under the pyramid
next to a heater. That means that the effect of
temperature is another thing that would have to
be taken into consideration when evaluating the
results of your experiment. If your glasses are
identical, the glass would be a constant, a factor
that would not have to be taken into consideration
until you tried another type of glass, when it would
become a variable. If you use blue blades in an
experiment, the type of blade is a constant, but
if you use a blue blade for the test and a stainless
steel for the control, the type of blade is a variable.
This means that a scientist could say that the
results may have more to do with the difference

in the type of blade used than in the fact that a pyramid was used to cover one. The essence of a good controlled experiment is reducing the variables to a minimum. This isn't easy to do in home experiments. If your wife, husband, child, or pet knocks one part of your experiment askew midway through, that becomes a variable that has to be taken into account when reaching your conclusions.

Variables get to be a real pain when testing pyramid effects on humans because humans are so variable within themselves and between each other. A man's beard grows at different rates during a month, and diet can affect the oiliness of his skin, which would affect the pull of the blade, and these become variables which have to be considered. The tasting ability of people varies widely, especially between smokers and non-smokers, and this certainly affects any conclusions you might draw from the reactions of people to a taste test. There are two ways to help overcome this difficulty. One is to extend the time of the experiment so that variables tend to cancel themselves out. Running a razor blade experiment for two weeks is not as valid as running one for four months. It is not uncommon for a person to get 120 shaves from a blue blade kept under a pyramid, but try to get the same, or anywhere near the same, without the pyramid. True, one person, because of the nature of his skin and beard, might only get 50 shaves, another only 90, but compared to the usual 7 to 10, this is highly significant.

Another way to reduce the importance of variables is to multiply the number of test subjects. Trying the taste test on two people is not very convincing, but when twenty-five, fifty or a hundred people try the test and 75 percent of them report a difference in taste, then you can be more sure of your results.

## *I have heard of a blind test. What is that?*

A blind test is one in which the subject, a person used in an experiment, doesn't know which is the test and which is the control. If you are testing for taste and you want to run a blind test, you will put the subject in another room and bring him the control glass and the test glass without letting him know which is which. That makes his reaction more valid because he doesn't have any subconscious preconceptions about how he is supposed to react.

## *Is a double-blind test the same thing?*

No, a double-blind test is intended to eliminate the possibility that the experimenter might be giving the subject some unconscious clues, like holding one glass a little forward of the other or looking expectant when he tries the test glass. The scientists who devised this were afraid that the subject would try to please the experimenter even without consciously wanting to. So in this case, the person carrying out the experiment with the subject doesn't even know which is the test and which is the control. He uses someone else to carry out his experiment. At home you could do this with three rooms. In one you would have your pyramid with the water under it and the control glass. Then you would take both glasses into the second room and leave them there while you return to the first room. Of course, you would have marked them in some way so only you would know which was which. Then your Aunt Agatha would come into the second room and carry them out to your Uncle Wolfgang (the subject) in the third room, where he would taste them. Agatha would note his reactions and then call you out so you could delightedly say, "See, I told you!" Or be disappointed and try again.

*Is there any other reason for experimenting besides proving something to myself?*

Yes! You will not merely be repeating what others have done, exciting as that can be. The field of pyramid energy is so new that it is wide open to new ideas and new kinds of tests. Just by working at home you could discover something that everyone else has overlooked. As this is being written, the news has come out that an amateur astronomer in Japan with a small telescope has discovered a new comet missed by all the hundreds of professional astronomers around the world using the best and most refined equipment. And people have been scanning the skies for centuries. Nearly every month I receive a letter from someone who has found out something new about pyramids, and every week people give me new ideas about experiments that I haven't the time to follow up. The knowledge is there, and the more people we have working with pyramids, the sooner we will know more about them and be able to apply that knowledge more effectively. Even mistakes can lead to new information and new uses.

### What about people who refuse to believe you even after your experiments show it works?

Your experimental work will give you more confidence in discussing pyramid energy with people, but don't waste time trying to break down unbreakable barriers. You will meet four kinds of people when the subject comes up, not including those who have experimented with it like you. First are those who will believe anything you say about it without checking. They are a bore. Then there are the healthy skeptics, who are the best of the lot. The 19th-century science they were taught in school (and it is still being taught) doesn't prepare them for the fact that a piece of cardboard can exhibit properties not usually associated with cardboard, but they are still willing to be shown whether or not it is true. They will question you sharply, and you had better know your subject and be honest about not knowing what you don't know. However, if they experience the effects of the energy, they won't be afraid to acknowledge it. Next are the brick-heads. Anything that goes outside of the bounds of what they already know is false, stupid, and probably dangerous. They can set your teeth on edge and had best be avoided. The worst of the four are the pseudo-intellectuals. They will undermine your confidence by quoting a dozen theories either stating that pyramids can't work or that the effects are due to something other than pyramids. They won't experiment, however, because that might upset their theories.

Do your experiments, draw your own conclusions, compare them with what others say or have written, and then, while the devout believers are just oohing and aahing, the brick-heads are running away, and the pseudo-intellectuals are looking smug, go out and *use* the stuff for your benefit.

# Chapter 4

# PYRAMIDS AND PLANTS

Now we get into the real meat of the matter. In this chapter we will discuss the effects of pyramids on plants and give you guidelines for setting up your own experiments. So, on with the questions!

*What effects do pyramids have on plants?*

That's a big question, but to generalize, pyramids enhance or stimulate seed germination and growth in some cases and retard germination and growth in others. They may also modify the direction of later plant growth and either increase crop yield or diminish it.

*That sounds contradictory.*
*I thought pyramids were only good for plants.*

Too much of the popular literature on pyramids would have you believe that they are the answer to all the ills of mankind and that they never are anything but good for you or your plants. The truth is that pyramids "generate" (a term I'll use for convenience, if you don't mind) energy, and that's all. In the case of plants, the energy generated by a particular pyramid may be just what the plant needs, not enough, or too much. You see, plants are sensitive to the energy in different ways, depending on the kind of plant and its size. Some plants can absorb and need a great deal of energy, while others are easily overloaded. Usually, the larger the plant, the more energy it can take.

*How do you know how much*
*energy to give a plant?*

By testing. You have to test each plant to see what its tolerance level is. It's possible that individual plants of the same species will react differently, though the tolerance level should be about the same. The fact is that not enough experiments have been done to be sure. In testing, I would recommend starting out with small dosages of energy and gradually building up until you find the best dosage for that particular plant. There is no sense in burning out your best begonia before you begin.

*What do you mean by a "dosage of energy?"*

Since there is no standard measurement for energy intensity, we have to define "dosage" in this context as "exposure time." In other words, you might treat a plant for 5 minutes, or 10, or half an hour or more. As long as you don't change your energy source, you have a roughly constant means of measuring dosage. Five minutes is a good starting dose, but let your own judgment prevail.

*Can you really burn out a plant?*

Yes. At least, that is the appearance. It is a result of overdose. A small overdose will cause a plant to wilt. This can happen anywhere from 1 to 12 hours after the treatment. The next stage of overdose, if the plant has received more than a wilting amount of energy, is a browning at the top. Then the plant will develop a burned appearance from the top downward. This is the extreme, of course. In practice it is rarely encountered unless you leave a weak plant in a strong field for a long time. The main thing you have to note is that an overdose is not necessarily fatal to your plant. It will usually recover from the wilting stage if you take it out of the field and let it recuperate.

*How do you apply the energy to the plant?*

The easiest way is to place it under a pyramid. The larger the plant, the larger the pyramid you will require, and the less exposure time until you determine its tolerance. A wire or wood framework pyramid will let you work with a lot more different-sized plants because it doesn't matter whether they have branches or leaves sticking out beyond the sides. If you have a solid-side pyramid, you can suspend it over the plant for treatment. This way a small pyramid, such as one 6 inches high, will serve for almost all your needs.

### *Are there any materials for pyramids that are better than others in treating plants?*

There isn't enough information yet to be absolutely certain, but based on my own experience I tend to think that plants will react better to pyramids made of organic materials. This would include cardboard, wood, and plastic. Metal pyramids seem to be too potent, though they are often helpful. The difference is very subtle, and is more of a feeling than an established fact. But we are dealing with life energy, and feelings are important to consider. Nevertheless, don't let me discourage you from trying metal. Experiment, and find out for yourself.

### *What about pyramid greenhouses?*

I think you will find that if you choose the right kind of plants, they will thrive beautifully in a pyramid greenhouse. You will have to discover which are the right ones by trial and error, because you will also find that some plants cannot take the constant inflow of energy. However, the greenhouse can also be used as a plant hospital where you can place ailing plants temporarily for a little "juicing up."

## Do you always have to put plants under a pyramid for treatment?

In this field you don't always have to do anything. Stay flexible. Another way to treat plants is to put them over a pyramid. Remember the grid that was mentioned in Chapter 1. You can set your plant right on a pyramid grid or on a bench over a larger single pyramid and still get effects. This is a good area for research, because very little controlled testing has been done. With plants over a pyramid, the roots are getting the primary dose of energy, and it would be very interesting to see whether this has a better or worse effect than treating it from the top. Also, the material and thickness of the bench and/or pot might be important to the effects of the energy.

## You said that a pyramid could be suspended over a plant. How high?

I'd suggest the minimum height at which an extended invisible pyramid would still cover the main part of the plant (see Fig. 6.) As you recall, a suspended pyramid seems to act like the tip of a larger pyramid, with energy effects within the invisible area. But while this "unseen pyramid" gets larger the higher you suspend the physical one, it does not follow that the energy output also increases the way it would with a larger physical pyramid. The fact is that it gets weaker, until no

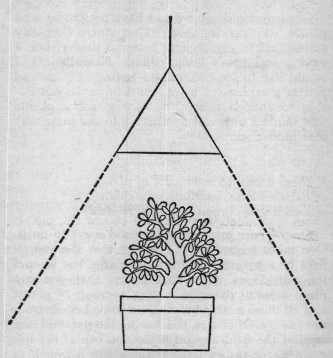

Suspended pyramid and invisible extension

Figure 6

effects can be detected. That's really too bad because otherwise we might be able to suspend a pyramid from a satellite and treat the whole earth. Ah, well. At any rate, keep to the minimum practical height for best effects.

## Would glass work for a pyramid greenhouse?

Glass pyramids do work. I have personally seen plants thriving in them. That doesn't exactly correspond to my organic material theory, but it works, and that's what counts. Nevertheless, I would like to see comparison testing of glass and plastic greenhouses in pyramid form. If you decide to undertake this, be sure to use a plastic that inhibits ultraviolet radiation in the same way that glass does.

## Is there a way to treat a lot of plants at once without building a greenhouse or suspending a pyramid over each plant?

Sure! There are two other good ways to do it. One takes advantage of the fact that the energy field of a pyramid is not only inside, but around the outside as well. That means that you can place a small pyramid among a group of plants and all those near it will receive some benefit from the energy. Of course, the smaller the pyramid, the smaller the field around it. So you can either use a couple of rather large pyramids or a bunch of smaller ones, depending on the number and arrangement of the plants you want to treat. As a *very* rough guide, you can estimate an effective field extending for about 6 to 12 inches around a 4-inch-high pyramid, and for about 1 to 2 feet around a 6-inch-high pyramid. Since the field around the pyramid is not as intense as the field inside, you may find that you can leave the pyramids in place without any overdose effects. Only trial and error will tell you for sure, though.

The other way is to treat water under a pyramid

and use that for your plants. Water seems to absorb the energy to a great degree, to get "charged," so to speak. Many researchers agree that using pyramid-treated water results in almost the same effects as placing a pyramid over the plant. Besides the convenience of using treated water, there is the added advantage that the danger of energy overdose is practically nil. It appears that water will absorb a certain amount of energy and no more, and that it will hold the absorbed amount for an indefinite period. So water makes a good medium for transferring energy to a plant or to a whole garden where direct pyramid treatment is not practicable.

*How long do you have to treat
water before it is fully charged?*

Reports vary, but I generally recommend about 15 minutes for every 8 ounces (one cup). That would make half an hour per pint and an hour per quart. These are *estimated* times that produce good results. They are not law. We may eventually find that the actual charging time is much shorter. Meanwhile, the above times are effective. You won't find much, if any, advantage in leaving the water to be charged for a longer period. After treatment, you can store the water and it will retain the charge.

*If pyramids are so good for plants,
why aren't the farmers rushing to build pyramids
in their fields or treat their irrigation water?*

In the first place, you have to realize that this field is very young, adequate reporting on pyramid results is very scarce, and farmers are among the most conservative people in the world (and rightly so). It would cost a lot of money to build large pyramids and set up treatment systems for irrigation. If I were a farmer, I would certainly want a lot more proof that the results were going to be worth the effort. There are a few encouraging reports that extra-high yields have been achieved in some large-scale experimental crop projects, but I have not seen any detailed information about how the projects were carried out. As a farmer I would·want to see the most complete reporting possible and independent verification several times over before I would invest time and money in it. The place for such verification and reporting to start might be on experimental farms run by agricultural colleges, and they might get interested if enough home experimenters come up with positive results backed by good record-keeping.

*What is the percentage of increase in plant growth or crop yield when using pyramids?*

I can't give you a clear answer because it depends on too many things. For instance, the kinds of plants involved; length, intensity and form of treatment; climatic and soil conditions, etc. Reports I have seen range from 5 percent to 300 percent, but they are practically impossible to evaluate because of a lack of information about the conditions of the experiments.

*How does pyramid energy affect seeds?*

The most common claims are that treated seeds germinate faster and produce larger and healthier plants. On the other hand, seeds may also germinate more slowly and produce stunted plants. The critical factor here is the length of treatment. Also to be considered are the intensity of the energy field and the type of seed. An energy overdose will make for a poor showing. Another effect, however, may be that the seeds will remain fertile much longer than normal and that over a period of time the last-used seeds will do better than the first ones.

*Is it true that a pyramid will preserve cut flowers?*

Yes, in a way. What will happen is that the flower tends to mummify. It will retain its shape and texture and the petals will stay on long after you would expect them to fall off, but it will lose its color and become darker if you leave it under the pyramid long enough. Even a short treatment of your cut flowers under a pyramid will help them to keep their fresh look longer, though. You will probably get better results if you put the cut flowers in a glass or vase of water. Cut flowers normally last longer if they are kept in water, but the charged water will keep them longer still. You will also note that the water will not develop the usual unpleasant musty odor that occurs when you leave the plant in the same water over a period of days.

*Can pyramids be used for growing sprouts?*

This is one of the tastiest and most practical ways to use a pyramid. One researcher I know of claims an increase from 15 ounces to 17 ounces in her sprout crop since using a pyramid. Many researchers report that the sprouts grow more quickly and abundantly, that they taste better, that there is much less loss from rot and spoilage, and that they keep longer afterward.

If you are not familiar with sprouting, it refers to the process of germinating seeds such as alfalfa, mung beans, sunflower and soybeans. The sprouts are mixed with or used in place of salads when they are just a few inches long. At that stage they are highly nutritious. The great advantage of sprouts is that they are cheap and you can grow them yourself in your kitchen with only a jar and some water. In about three days you have a nice crop of fresh food. The simple process and short growing time make them ideal for pyramid experiments. You could try treating the seeds, treating the water, or treating the jars during the growth period. Most health food stores carry sprouting kits and books on sprouting. To insure a good controlled experiment, you will want to weigh out the seeds used for each experimental group.

## Will the pyramid keep insects away from plants?

There's a lot of *lalau* (that's Hawaiian for nonsense, mistaken notions, and deception) going around about the effect of pyramid energy on insects. Some people would have you believe that insects are of such a "low vibration" that they cannot stand the "higher vibrations" of pyramid energy. Here is a beautiful case of ignoring facts for the sake of a theory. The supporters of this theory have obviously not done any serious experimenting. The facts show that some insects apparently thrive on the energy while others don't care for it. They have about the same range of reactions as humans. Let me cite some examples.

In one experiment some grapes were cut in two. Half the grapes were placed in a bowl under a pyramid and half in a bowl in the open air. In 24 hours the grapes under the pyramid were full of fruit flies, but they left the open ones alone.

Another experiment was the result of my umbrella plant attracting a colony of aphids. The plant was treated overnight for several days in a strong field of pyramid energy. For the first couple of days it seemed as if there were fewer aphids and that those remaining were immobilized. But then they returned in strength, and continued charging didn't faze them at all.

On the other hand, there are *indications* that cockroaches don't particularly like the energy. This information is based on some personal experience and reports from others, but I'd like to stress that this is still in the realm of speculation, because no controlled testing has been done yet.

Recent plant research shows that the healthier a plant, the less likely it is to be bothered by insects. If the pyramid energy is actually improving the health of living plants, that in itself should help reduce insect problems. However, it has also been shown that plants have an emotional life similar to that of humans. Emotional stress can weaken a plant or a human so that they are more susceptible to disease or parasites, even if they are otherwise healthy. So it may be that my umbrella plant is upset about something. I'll have to talk to it.

*Is there any way to transfer pyramid energy
from one place to another besides through water?*

Yes, there is. In the first chapter I mentioned
that beams of energy come off the tip and corners
and that the energy has some of the characteristics
of electricity. These facts have been used by several researchers to draw energy from the pyramid
and use it somewhere else. Usually, the energy
is drawn off the tip, but success has also been reported by drawing energy from the lower corners
as well.

Most often it is done by attaching a wire to the
tip or corner and connecting the other end to a
metal plate or rod. Copper is the favored material
for the wire because it is a good electrical con-
ductor. However, pyramid energy doesn't pay
much attention to the rules of electricity; we have
found that ordinary string will conduct the energy,
too. Still, it does seem as if copper amplifies the
potency of the energy and this makes it very easy
to give the plant an overdose. It is known, for
instance, that a quick way to kill a tree is to drive
copper nails into the base. My advice is to use
copper sparingly with plants.

*Has this technique been used with plants?*

Yes, and with quite interesting results. In one
case, a copper wire was attached to a pyramid
at one end of a garden, then run a few inches
underground for the length of the plot and attached to another pyramid at the other end. Radish
seeds were planted over the wire and a control
row was planted some distance away. To the sur-

prise of the researcher, the plants over the wire did very poorly, either not germinating or being stunted. The control group grew very well. I think this shows the effects of an overdose.

Another type of experiment used a pyramid sitting outside and a wire leading down into a basement. There it was attached to a metal plate stuck in a pot with a plant. Control plants were also used. According to the report, the controls were white and sickly, while the treated plant grew healthy and *green*, as if photosynthesis were taking place without the sun. To be fair, I have not seen complete reports on this, nor do I know whether it has been duplicated. There's something else for you to try!

*Will you describe a simple plant experiment that anyone can try?*

Sure. Here's one that should be easy to reproduce:

Take a package of radish seeds for this experiment. I suggest radish seeds because the growing time is short. Use half the seeds for the test and half for the control. To prepare for the experiment, get two trays or wooden flats about 18"x27". The exact size isn't important as long as they are both the same and made out of the same material. Prepare enough soil to fill both trays, mixing it thoroughly so that both trays get soil as nearly the same as possible. Place the trays as far apart as you can while still keeping the amount of sunlight, air circulation, and other environmental factors the same. Six feet ought to be a minimum to make sure you don't get a carry-over effect from the pyramid field. To reduce another possible variable, align both trays with their length along the line of magnetic north.

Over one tray, place the pyramid of your choice. Either a framework pyramid that covers the whole tray or a small enclosed pyramid (open bottom) suspended from a crossbar over the tray would probably be best. Naturally, the pyramids should be properly aligned. Now make your rows and plant an equal number of seeds in each tray. When you water, measure it out so that each tray receives an equal amount. In your notebook, make a careful record of everything you do, and record the results from day to day at the same hour even if nothing seems to be happening. For the daily record-keeping, also note the climate and temperature at the time you make your entry.

It's your choice as to how long you want to run the experiment. You might just want to see how long it takes for the plants to break through the soil. Or you might fix a certain number of days for the experiment and see whether there is any difference in growth within that time. You can also continue it until the radishes mature and test them for differences in taste, size, quantity, and weight.

As an alternate experiment, which would take up less space, since you won't have to have the trays so far apart, you can just treat the seeds or just treat the water. If you treat the seeds only, charge them for 24 hours before planting, leaving the control seeds alone, of course. Why 24? It's a good arbitrary number that's easy to control, and you'll know your seeds will have been well-charged. However, feel free to try any time limit you choose. If you treat the water only, draw an equal amount as a control and leave it out for the same length of time that you keep the test water under the pyramid.

Running an experiment just once doesn't prove very much to skeptics because they can always say it was a fluke. So, the more times you can run the same experiment the better. Since you will probably be interested in proving the effects of pyramid energy more to yourself and your friends than to the scientific community, I'd suggest that you do the same experiment at least three times in order for your results to have real meaning. *Then*, you can do the world a great favor by typing up your notes and either publishing them yourself or sending them to someone who can use them in research (like me!). Whether you take the time to do that or not, I still hope you experiment. As investigation spreads, so will knowledge and improvements.

### *How about some more types of experiments to do?*

Without going into a lot of detail, here are a few ideas to stimulate your thinking: Test two pyramid-covered radish trays with one tray's long side north and south and the other east and west. Do the same thing but with one pyramid aligned and the other not. Test the benefits of direct pyramid energy against pyramid-treated water. If you have a little electrical talent, you might want to test galvanic responses of plants with and without pyramids or attempt a bit of Kirlian photography on leaves from treated and untreated plants. One report states that electrophotographs show an increase in corona size when a cut leaf has been treated under a pyramid. For more fun you could see whether some seeds or plants respond better to pyramid energy than others. Radishes versus lettuce, for example. Such a list as this could go on and on, but I think you have the idea now.

## TROUBLESHOOTING

There will be times when you think you've done everything right and still the experiment doesn't turn out right. I don't necessarily mean that it doesn't turn out the way you expected—nature is full of surprises—but that you don't get comparative results. Below we'll list some possible problems and their probable causes.

*The plants under my pyramid wilted.* More than likely it's an overdose. You may have left the pyramid over the plants for too long, or those particular plants may be supersensitive. Try a shorter treatment period.

*There wasn't any difference between the test plants under the pyramid and the control.* It's a common problem. The first thing you want to do is check the orientation of your pyramid. If that's okay, then you want to check the distance of your control from the pyramid. If it is too close, it may be absorbing the pyramid energy, too. Should that be okay, you do have a problem. One thing to do is wait a week and try again in case the cause is meteorological in origin. Another thing is to check to see whether there are a lot of electrical appliances, transformers, or power lines nearby.

Unlike some researchers who think electrical equipment damps out the pyramid effects, I think they amplify it and produce similar effects of their own. So if both test and control plants are being swamped by energy, you probably won't be able to tell the difference caused by a pyramid, especially a small one. A third thing is to move the experiment to another location. I can't go into details in this book, but there are energy-amplifying and energy-sapping spots on the earth, and in certain locations these could conceivably affect your experiment. If absolutely nothing changes the situation. go back to raising hamsters.

*My plants always increase in size when I do the experiment, but when my (wife, husband, friend, lover) does it they don't.* You might as well know it now. Plants are telepathic. No kidding, they can sense or respond to your emotions and expectations. If you strongly expect and desire your plants to do better under a pyramid they will, but a "desire to please" will have a lot to do with it. On the other hand, a very negative attitude can cause an opposite reaction in plants. They are still responding to expectations, but this time in spite of the pyramid energy. Try to be as neutral as possible about the results.

*The control plants did better than the test ones.* Sounds like another case of overdose. Try a shorter treatment period.

It's amazing that more experiments haven't been done with pyramid energy and plants. The area is wide open and could have important implications for such fields as market gardening. Perhaps this chapter will stimulate one of you out there to become a pyramid-oriented plant wizard à la Luther Burbank. I wish you all the best.

# Chapter 5

# PYRAMIDS AND FOODS

The earliest pyramid energy experiments were done with food, or at least with flesh, since a dead cat was used in one of them. As you remember from Chapter 1, André Bovis carried out mummification experiments right after getting back from Egypt. These were successfully duplicated by other researchers in France, Czechoslovakia, and later in the U.S. Testing the effects of pyramids on food is one of the easiest and most enjoyable ways of experimenting. Ready for question one.

*How does the pyramid mummify meat?*

By a dehydration process that drives out the water molecules, as far as can be determined now. In early experiments with hamburger, I noticed that the portions of meat kept under the pyramid developed beads of water on the surface or on the support under them. This did not occur with the controls. The meat kept under the pyramids shrank in size, became very hard, did not spoil, and developed no odor. I have to admit, however, that sometimes the controls turned out the same way, though without the water beading and perhaps not quite as much weight loss. Still, they did not spoil nor did they smell. After going crazy over variables for a while I finally realized that the climate in Southern California does get very dry at times. In fact, mummification is a common process in deserts all over the world without pyramids. It is the presence of water that provides breeding conditions for bacteria that cause spoilage. So it would seem that the pyramid stimulates rapid evaporation in the same way, if not by the same method, that dry air and the sun do. It takes energy to evaporate water, and the mummification effect of pyramids shows that energy is at work. Keep in mind that your mummification experiments with a pyramid will be more dramatic in a more humid climate than that of Southern California. If you live in the Golden State, I suggest you carry out your mummification experiments in the bathroom (unless you want to dehydrate a dead cat). That should be the most humid place in the house. In choosing the kind of meat you are going to mummify, you should also take into account the fact that much of our food today is stuffed with chemical preservatives, which could confuse your research results.

*Will the meat still be edible after mummification?*

Yes, it will. Meat has been kept under pyramids

for several months without spoilage, and it still tastes good—sometimes even tastier because of the concentration due to dehydration. I recently talked to some people who are using pyramids to make good beef jerky for home use. It is only a matter of time before it becomes commercialized.

### Can you put any amount of meat in a pyramid to mummify?

You can do it, but your results won't be so hot if the quantity of meat is too large in relation to the pyramid. The available energy in a pyramid depends on its size and, to a certain extent, the material it is made of. I know someone who put a pound of hamburger under a 6-inch-high cardboard pyramid and was extremely disappointed that it didn't mummify overnight. If left in such a pyramid for any length of time, the meat will certainly spoil, simply because there isn't enough energy to prevent it. For that kind of pyramid I recommend an ounce or less of meat and give it at least a week. For a shorter experiment, use less meat. In my first experiments I used a ball of raw hamburger about a quarter-inch in diameter and got my results in 3 days.

### Does it matter where you locate the meat in the pyramid?

There is some controversy over this, but my records definitely indicate the greatest effect at the King's Chamber position, about a third of the way up from the base of the pyramid. Let me put it this way: the dehydration effect is more active at that point than anywhere else in the structure.

*Can any kind of meat be used?*

All kinds of meat have been mummified under pyramids, the best results being obtained from those with the greatest moisture content.

*Do fruits mummify under a pyramid also?*

It might be better to say that they undergo dehydration. As with meat, the more moisture content to begin with, the greater the dehydration. I used an apple to first demonstrate the King's Chamber effect. In a very carefully controlled 72-hour experiment with apple wedges placed outside and at various points within 6-inch cardboard pyramids, the piece at the King's Chamber, or "phi point," as I like to call it, showed the greatest reduction in size, the most weight loss, and the least discoloration. Verne Cameron, an early researcher, reported that he placed a large hunk of watermelon under a small pyramid for several days and that it shrank to the size of an apricot while still retaining its sweetness and flavor.

*Is dehydration the only effect*
*pyramids have on fruit?*

No, there is also a preservative effect, and a taste enhancement effect, and a ripening effect. When you buy fruit—or vegetables—and treat them under the pyramid for about half an hour before putting them away, they will tend to stay fresh longer. Fruit that doesn't need refrigeration can be left under a framework pyramid in a bowl until it is eaten. In one experiment we left an apple under a pyramid for 3 months and it was still fresh, unspoiled, and tasty inside. Of course, the length of time and quality of preservation depend on a lot of variables like the kind of fruit, the temperature and humidity, air currents, and so on. Nevertheless, overall the preservation of fruits and vegetables does seem to be enhanced by a pyramid, apparently by inhibiting bacterial action.

*What did you mean by "taste enhancement"?*

Just that the pyramid often makes food taste better. How it does that is a good question for debate. Two possible reasons are currently popular. One is the idea that the pyramid energy stimulates the action of enzymes, which affect taste. The other is that the dehydration causes a concentration of taste. At any rate, it works. One of my favorite ways to use this effect is on avocados. Because avocados are picked when hard and undeveloped, they do not benefit from the tree juices as they soften in your refrigerator or on your shelf. So although they may become soft, they might as well be made of cardboard as far as taste goes. But when I cut them and leave them under a pyramid for 10 to 30 minutes they develop a real avocado taste. This will work with virtually any food, including meat and vegetables. The ripening effect is closely related and seems to work best when the food is left overnight under the pyramid, or longer if the fruit is really hard. Try it with avocados, bananas, peaches, and similar hard-picked fruit.

*How does the energy act with citrus fruit?*

I can only cite one full-fledged experiment in this regard. We squeezed the juice of a fresh lemon into a cup and had it tasted by several subjects. Most noticeable by all was a very pungent smell in addition to the sour taste. A control cup of juice was also used, and it exhibited the same characteristics. The test cup was placed under a 6-inch-high pyramid and the control a good distance away. After a half-hour the control didn't seem any different, but the test cup had lost the pungent smell. After two hours, the test cup of juice was definitely less sour than the control, as verified by all the subjects. It was still sour, but not nearly as much as before the test.

*Have you tried it with eggs?*

I haven't, but Mankind Research Unlimited of Washington, D.C., has. They were mainly trying to test for the existence of an energy within the pyramid that might be different from other shapes or open air. What they did was to break an egg on a plate and put one in a pyramid, one within a cube, and one in the open air. I read the research results and saw the photos showing the eggs after 3 weeks, if I remember right. The egg under the pyramid looked almost fresh, the one in the open air was slightly spoiled, and the one in the cube looked worst of all.

*Is there any effect on milk?*

Generally, milk treated under a pyramid will

stay fresh longer. One of these days a milk carton manufacturer will make a fortune by making cartons with pyramid-shaped tops. Remember that the energy flows downward below the pyramid, so the whole carton would not have to be in a pyramid shape, which would make it awkward for your refrigerator. You can test the effect on milk by getting 2 half-pints of milk with the same expiration date, then putting one directly into the refrigerator and the other under a pyramid for a half-hour test. Test by smell and taste after the due date.

It has also been said that milk kept under a pyramid will not spoil, but will develop into cheese. According to the reports (I have not tried this myself) the milk has to be left 4 to 5 weeks, during which it develops a crust, a layer of liquid, and the cheese below. On the other hand, I also have reports from people who say that it doesn't work. I suspect it depends a lot on the type or brand of milk used. Some of it is full of preservatives, and that would certainly affect the experiment. If you want to try it, be sure to use proper experimental procedures and remember that even the same brand can be a variable.

*Is it true that a pyramid will*
*take the bitterness out of coffee?*

This time I can give an unqualified yes! It is one of the easiest and most dramatic tests to perform. Make your coffee and let it cool enough to drink. Taste it, then put it under the pyramid for a few minutes and taste it again. Unless your taste buds have been dulled by heavy drinking or smoking, you will notice a definite mellowing of the coffee. Some people claim it tastes sweeter, others blander. Over hundreds of taste experiments I have found that the thing to test for is a *difference* between the treated and untreated liquid, rather than a specific effect. I never fully realized until doing these experiments just how subjective taste really is.

*You said a "few minutes."*
*Can't you be more definite?*

Nope. It all depends on the size of your pyramid, the bitterness of your coffee, and the sensitivity of your own taste buds. However, I almost always get a reaction from people after 5 to 10 minutes with a 6-inch-high cardboard pyramid.

*Will it work with tea, as well?*

Yes, it will. Again, the result will be to make the tea taste smoother. There have also been very successful results with wine. You may have heard the reports, but I can verify that in my own experience a glass of inexpensive wine treated under the pyramid for about a half-hour tastes more like an aged wine worth much more. The harshness has softened and the bouquet has improved. I have been asked what would happen if a good wine were put under the pyramid. Nothing noticeable, I can assure you, at least as far as taste is concerned. The wine undoubtedly picks up a charge, but not enough testing has been done to determine with any certainty the effect of that charge. It is my personal opinion that pyramid energy acts on alcohol in such a way as to lessen its effects on the human system, but I stress that this is only an opinion based on preliminary research.

### Are there effects on other kinds of drinks?

Yes, but they are not always what you would call beneficial. For instance, apple cider left under a pyramid will lose its tartness. If you like your cider tart, this is a disadvantage. Also, the pyramid will cause carbonated beverages to go flat faster. So far, all carbonation tests have been done with open glasses or bottles. No one has tried, or reported any results from, testing with sealed bottles.

### Does pyramid energy work with dry tea or coffee?

Right! You can treat a whole pound under a pyramid and have it all come out tasting more mellow. But in this case I would recommend leaving it under the pyramid overnight.

### I've read that it works on tobacco, too.

Well, here we have some difficulty. I've read that myself, but my results are inconclusive. I've tried it on my pipe tobacco, and I have to honestly say that I can't tell any difference. Some friends who are cigarette smokers say it works; others say it doesn't. We are in an area where types of tobacco, individual taste, and control conditions all play an important part. Tobacco itself varies in taste with humidity and blends and age. To sum it up, I have not seen any results that show reasonable scientific reporting, so the conclusions are still up in the air.

*Does it do anything to plain water?*

Chlorinated and mineralized tap water will lose the chlorine and mineral taste after a short time under a pyramid. Some people like the difference, comparing it to fresh spring water, while others prefer the tap water, saying the pyramid water tastes too bland. But nearly everyone does taste a difference. In this kind of testing it is very necessary to use a control. Some experimenters have gotten mistaken results because they didn't know that tap water left open for a while will lose its chlorine by a natural process without a pyramid. As in other areas, the pyramid seems to speed up what comes naturally. Some people like to leave a glass of water in the pyramid overnight and drink it in the morning, claiming that it energizes them.

*Someone told me that the pyramid
purifies the water. Is that so?*

There are those who let their desires run ahead of their common sense, or who are sloppy about the use of words. "To purify" means to remove impurities. So far there is no indication that pyramid energy takes anything out of the water that would not leave by itself anyway, such as the chlorine. I have a second-hand report of experiments done in Europe which seem to show that the pyramid energy alters the molecular structure of the water, which could change the effects of impurities. However, I have not been able to obtain copies of the original report, and I do know that scientists are still debating about what the molecular structure of water really is (not the composition but the structure). Because of the effects of pyramid water on plants and skin (to be covered in a later chapter) I think it is fairly safe to say that the pyramid *adds* something to the water. But it is very inaccurate in the light of present knowledge to say that the pyramid "purifies" the water. Considering the dehydration effect of pyramid energy we can assume that it speeds up the evaporation process, though how this affects taste and structure is anybody's guess at this stage.

### Has the pyramid been used as a storage device for large quantities of food?

Well, a growing number of people are using fairly large pyramids for the storage of dried foods such as grains, certain fruits and vegetables, and items like cookies and candies. These are usually covered pyramids with a 3- to 6-foot base. They claim the food stays fresh, that it tastes better after storage, and that they seldom have trouble with insects. One report given to me states that a family successfully replaced their refrigerator with a pyramid for a period of six months. I don't know what they did after that.

### What will the pyramid do to honey?

From two different sources I read that honey would act in strange ways under a pyramid. You were supposed to place the honey in a rectangular dish aligned north and south and place a pyramid over it. In 3 days the honey was supposed to turn stiff and tacky. Then the pyramid was to be taken out of alignment for 24 hours and the honey would turn soft again. If you put the pyramid back into alignment it was supposed to turn tacky again in 3 days. From the accounts this could be kept up indefinitely.

So I set up the experiment. I aligned the honey in a long glass dish and placed a 6-inch-high cardboard pyramid over it, also aligned. Nothing happened after 3 days, so I let it sit. Seven days later the honey did seem tackier, and I put the pyramid out of alignment. I tried again after 24 hours, but there was no difference. It took 3 days for the honey to turn soft again. I put the pyramid back in alignment and waited another 7 days, testing occasionally in between. The honey had turned reasonably tacky, and once more I disaligned the pyramid. This time it took 5 days for it to become soft. On impulse I took the pyramid off to see what would happen. In only 48 hours it had turned tackier than ever. At this point I dropped the experiment, as the results did not show that any pyramid action was taking place. Something was affecting the honey, but it could have been anything from temperature to moon phases. The fault with this experiment was that I had not set up a control, another dish of honey which I could have compared to the test dish. Instead of getting results, I got confused. Please don't make the same mistake that I did in this case.

### Is it true that the pyramid will eliminate artificial flavors?

To test this idea I tried to duplicate a candy experiment I read about in another report. That report said that hard candy of several flavors was treated in a pyramid for one hour. In a double-blind test a panel of subjects picked flavors out of a bowl at random and tried to identify the flavors by taste. The subjects were blindfolded and did not know what flavors to expect. Eight out of ten could not correctly identify the flavor. The only two who did had picked peppermint.

For this experiment I did use controls. I bought two sets of four flavors: cherry, grape, lemon, and orange. All were wrapped in cellophane. One of each kind was placed under a 6-inch cardboard pyramid for 24 hours, and the other set was left on a shelf in another room. The subjects knew there were four flavors, but not what kind they were. As it was, I only used three flavors, lemon, cherry, and grape.

Seven subjects were used in the first double-blind test. The purpose of the test was to taste two different pieces of candy and try to detect any flavor differences, as far as the subjects were concerned. Unknown to them, both pieces were labeled as lemon, one being from the pyramid and the other from the control group. I think it worthwhile to note their taste reactions in chart form.

| SUBJECT | TEST CANDY | CONTROL CANDY |
|---|---|---|
| #1 | lemon | grape, sweeter |
| #2 | stale lemon, flat | bittersweet lemon, more taste |
| #3 | lemon, sweeter | lemon, less tasty |
| #4 | lemon | lemon, sweeter |
| #5 | lemon | grape, sweeter |
| #6 | grape, sweeter | sour orange, grape aftertaste |
| #7 | orange, sweet & sour | barely any flavor |

This test tells us several things. First, some subjects apparently don't know the difference between lemon and grape. Actually, it is probable that artificial flavors rely much more on color to enhance their taste than is generally realized. The second thing brought out by the test is that taste is a highly individual phenomenon. The subjects can't even agree on intensity of taste, or degree of sweetness or sourness. Finally, it shows that even 24 hours in a pyramid was not enough to eliminate artificial flavors. There does seem to have been some slight alteration in flavor, but not enough to justify the claim that pyramid energy does away with "artificiality."

The next test took place a full week later. Five subjects were involved, and the results were more consistent. The flavors were grape and cherry, and all subjects except one agreed that the control candy had more taste. That one thought the test candy was more tasty. I like to use her as a subject because she usually has opposite reactions to everyone else and that helps to keep our heads straight. Although the test candy had been in the pyramid all week, none of the subjects had any difficulty in guessing which flavors were involved. The taste wasn't as pronounced, but it was still there. Since all the artificial flavors contained citric acid, I suspect that the energy is acting to neutralize this acid, as in the lemon juice experiment, rather than affecting the artificial flavors as such.

The last test in this series had to do with odor. Eight subjects were asked to determine which of the candies—grape, cherry, and lemon—from both test and control groups smelled the strongest. This was also a double-blind test. All agreed that the test cherry smelled stronger, three thought that the control grape was stronger, and all agreed that the control lemon was stronger. This jolted our expectations all to pieces, and I just don't know what to make of it without a lot more testing.

The conclusion to make from all of this is that the pyramid energy is doing *something* to the candy, but it is premature to say exactly what. I do not think we are justified in saying that anything "artificial" is automatically neutralized by the energy, because the word *artificial* is a cultural concept. Too many people associate "artificial" with "bad," but that is pure unthinking prejudice. Plastic, chemical flavors, synthetic cloth and cars are artificial in the sense that they are manmade objects not found in nature. But then so are dyed cotton cloth, saddles on horses, wooden houses . . . and pyramids.

## Can you give us some guidelines for a food experiment?

Okay. Let's do a coffee taste test as an example. Remember that the main effect is to remove or reduce the bitterness, so you don't want to use the finest grade of coffee available (unless you want to use it as a second control to see how closely your pyramidized cheap coffee approaches it in mellowness). If you are going to use a number of different subjects at different times, be sure to stick to the same brand, preferably from the same jar or can. To cut down on variables, you will also want to use the same kind of cup for all the experiments. Glass, china, and plastic all work well, but for the purposes of experimenting use a single kind. Use cold water from the same source and make your coffee. Set your coffee under whatever kind of pyramid you have chosen for your experiment and place the control cup a good distance away. Decide on your charging period. Five minutes is good. Now, for a simple test, just taste each one and see what you think. To get more complicated, blindfold yourself and have someone else give you the cups to taste. And to get really difficult, get someone else to give the cups to another person who doesn't know where they came from who can then give them to you. You can play the same game with other people. To return to simplicity, you can merely use one cup and taste it before and after treating it under the pyramid, but this wouldn't have as much "scientific validity," even though you could tell the difference.

## Isn't this a very subjective experiment?

Naturally, since it involves individual taste. But when you concentrate on the *difference* between treated and untreated coffee rather than on a specific taste sensation, you are dealing with more objective results. By the way, I'm going to let you in on a little secret. In general, the only difference between an "objective" result and a "subjective" one is that the former is based on the sense of sight and the latter on some other sense. What we have to deal with is that our society sets a high priority on the sense of sight, to the point where it is supposed to result in truer perception than do the other senses. Winetasters wouldn't agree, nor would many people who have listened to witnesses on jury duty. To further confuse you, a significant body of scientists are of the opinion that there is no such thing as an objective experiment—the mere presence or attention of the experimenter modifies the experiment. So don't worry overmuch about objectivity or subjectivity. If you can see, feel, taste, or smell a difference in your experiment, that's what counts. No one else can sense for you.

## TROUBLESHOOTING

The potential problem in food experiments are quite obvious, so we won't spend too much time on them. If the experiment doesn't work, check on orientation, relative size of the pyramid and test object, and whether you allowed the introduction of too many variables. In the case of taste tests, remember that some people have a poor sense of taste due to smoking, drinking, or colds. When trying to duplicate other people's experiments, you'll find that so many things were left out of their description that you will rarely get identical results. Just be happy if you come close.

# Chapter 6

# PYRAMIDS, PEOPLE, AND PETS

Humans and animals are interdependent with their environment. That's what the whole ecology movement is about. Whatever affects the environment affects us. We have shown that pyramids can have an effect on the environment, so it stands to reason that they can affect humans and animals as well. Let's take a look at this aspect of pyramid energy, starting with the animal kingdom.

*How do animals react to pyramids?*

In my experience, most seem to like it. I am speaking particularly of dogs and cats, having observed these more than others. If a pyramid is set up where it is accessible, a dog or cat will often pick it out as a preferred resting spot. On some occasions I have watched such an animal go within an open-frame pyramid and stay there for 5 or 10 minutes and then leave it, not going back until a day or two later. It is almost as if the animal is getting as much charge as it feels it needs, and doesn't return until it needs recharging again. Of course, this is speculation, since we don't know what is really going on inside the animal's head, but it does correspond to human reactions and may have validity. I have also known of sick dogs who sought out the pyramid and stayed there all day and night, leaving only to eat, until they felt—or at least acted as though they felt—better.

## Does the pyramid energy affect their diet?

I have heard two stories, one about a dog and the other about a cat, in which both were supposed to have stopped eating meat after regularly sleeping in a pyramid for a number of weeks. According to the stories, they became vegetarians and only took up meat again after the pyramids were taken away. I have to admit my extreme skepticism about these tales. They are apparently intended to promote the idea that the energy is so "purifying" that it will even make animals give up meat for food of a "higher vibration." Nothing in my four years of testing has indicated that pyramid energy does any such thing. It does a lot of things that could be called weird in some contexts, but causing vegetarianism is not one of them. If someone shows me convincing evidence, however, I'll be willing to look at it with an open mind, and then wonder why it doesn't affect humans in the same way.

## What about healing effects on animals?

From what I have been told, experiments are now underway at a major university to test the healing effects of pyramids on rats and mice. (By the way, the reason I do not name the university or university researchers is because they would prefer to remain anonymous until they get their results written up.) I have reports from people that tell of cuts on their pets being healed faster, or hair that had come out growing back in faster than normal, and of aged pets seemingly rejuvenated. These reports are from sincere people. They could hardly be called scientific, but neither should they be discounted.

## Can the energy calm down an angry or hyperactive pet?

Since bad-tempered animals are in a state of emotional anxiety, which is often picked up from their owners, I would think that the pyramid energy would help to relax the pet and allow for an easy discharge of the energy. This is another area where there has not been any controlled testing, and so we can only speculate. Nevertheless, I don't think that clomping a pyramid down over an angry pet is going to automatically and immediately make it peaceful. If it works, it will probably take a little while before any reaction to the energy will be noticed. A bit of excitement is a lot easier to calm down than full-blown anger, whether in a pet or in a human. One of my researchers recently reported that she placed a pyramid over the cage of an excitable bird. The bird immediately flew to the top of the cage in an apparent attempt to get as close to the pyramid as possible and has since remained far more calm than before.

## Do pets react to pyramid-treated water?

Very well, in my experience. When treated versus tap water was being tested with cats and dogs, they almost always took the treated water. Why *almost* always I don't know. Perhaps they already felt charged up that day, or perhaps there were unknown factors that altered the treated water on that occasion. At any rate, most of the time they preferred the treated. In another rather loose experiment, a friend of mine had two German Shepherds with a serious vomiting problem. It was so bad that he was reluctantly considering putting them away. I had him try treated water, and the results were remarkable. The vet had said nothing could be done because the dogs were vomiting several times a day. Within 2 weeks after using the treated water, one dog was down to vomiting once every other day, and the second dog only two or three times a week. Improvement continued after that. It has been two years, and as far as I know the dogs are still alive and well.

## How would you suggest getting a pet to try the pyramid?

For a caged pet like a hamster or a bird there is no problem because there is no choice. Just place or suspend the pyramid over the cage. If the cage is rather large, pick any spot you think is suitable. Try the sleeping section to see how the animal reacts, if you like.

For roaming animals like dogs and cats, I would suggest placing the pyramid on or over a favorite resting place. I would not suggest putting it right over the normal sleeping area until you see how the pet is going to react to it elsewhere. How would you feel if you came home to find that someone had built a pyramid over your bed and expected you to sleep under it without your knowing anything about it? Animals have habit patterns, too, and changing an established sleeping place can be upsetting. The change of a resting place is easier to accept. If, after a few days, it seems that the pet doesn't mind or actually enjoys the pyramid, then you might consider placing it over the sleeping area if you have a good reason for it like running an experiment or hoping to improve its health. Otherwise, your pet is better off having a choice in the matter of using the pyramid or not.

## What kinds of experiments can be run with pets?

It depends on how scientific you want to be. The ideal situation would be to have two groups of white rats or mice of known parentage in cages large enough to give them a choice of activity areas, yet small enough to be able to induce stress situations. One group would have no pyramids, and the other would have either a large pyramid covering the entire cage or smaller pyramids in various areas, depending on the nature of the experiment. Tests could be conducted and notations made on everything from comparative reactions to stress (crowding, pecking order, healing of wounds) to preferred living arrangements (nesting areas) to any differences in pregnancy and offspring. Since I suspect that few of you would have such facilities, a good home experiment could be carried out with a hamster in a fairly large cage with runs and several available nesting areas. Small pyramids could be placed over different areas to see whether they are preferred by the hamster or not. If the hamster happens to pick a spot under a pyramid for a nest, you could move the pyramid to another area to see whether it was the pyramid or the area itself that determined the choice. You could also offer two drinking spouts, one with regular and one with treated water, and check to see which is used more.

Less scientific, but just as much fun, are the experiments you can run for your own information on other pets. Here we are simply talking about offering regular and treated water and the choice of resting under a pyramid or not. For a little more interest, make a note of your pet's sleeping, eating, roaming, and emotional habits for a week or two before starting the experiments, and then keep a record after you start to see whether there are any changes.

## Could a pyramid affect fish?

In my opinion, yes. I have conducted extensive tests using devices that give off the same energy as a pyramid and have noted an increased lifespan and healing effects, as well as an initial retardation in algae growth in the aquarium, but I have not used the pyramid form in these experiments. I suspect I would get similar results, but I won't say for sure until I try it. So far as I know, there have been no experiments reported using pyramids with fish. However, experimenters Bill Kerrell and Kathy Goggin have reported that brine shrimp (popularly known as "sea monkeys") grow larger and live longer when raised under a pyramid. Brine shrimp are easy to obtain and raise—most toy stores have kits—and are ideal for simple, controlled experiments.

Now, let's move on to the people kingdom.

### *Do people have physical reactions to pyramids?*

Right. In Chapter 1 I described these briefly. Generally, people feel either heat or coolness, tingling, currents and a pressure or breeze-like sensation. The effects felt may vary for the same person at different times. The temperature phenomenon is curious because it doesn't seem to have anything to do with actual temperature—two people feeling the same pyramid at the same time may report completely different temperature sensations. Obviously something is being sensed which the body translates as temperature, though no one knows why it sometimes senses warmth and sometimes coolness. The tingling sensation most often occurs in the palm of the hands or the fingertips, but once in a while a person says he can feel it all over. It is something like the "pins and needles" feeling when the circulation picks up in a hand that has fallen asleep, but usually not as strong. The currents may appear in any part of the body, regardless of which part is in the pyramid. For instance, if you put your hand inside a small pyramid, it is possible to feel a current in your arm, along your back, in your leg, or anywhere else. It is hard to describe the current, but you

The author, Dr. Serge V. King, displays two forks he bent by mind-directed energy with the help of a pyramid. He claims the metal felt briefly like putty during the process.

A group of volunteers test the effects of meditating with cardboard pyramids. Most reported sensations of tingling and warmth.

**Top Left:** Dr. Lawrence Kennedy of Los Angeles and his son Chris **(Bottom)** have also bent metal under a pyramid using only mind-directed energy. **Above:** Pyramids are used to speed up germination and to enhance the growth of plants. Note the difference in size between the radishes under the pyramid and the rest of the rows. The pyramid was in place from the time the seeds were planted.

**Left:** A framework pyramid has virtually the same effects as an enclosed one. Meditating outdoors is felt by some to be better in terms of pyramid energy effects. **Below:** Notice the haze above the tip of the pyramid. The sky was overcast and the camera does not leak light. Was this an effect of pyramid energy?

**Top:** Even a six-inch pyramid suspended over a bed can have a beneficial effect on sleeping because the energy flows downward. This one is suspended from the wall by a tripod made from a stick and two pieces of string. **Bottom:** The author's children, Pierre and Dion, holding a cat under a pyramid. Children and animals seem to enjoy pyramid energy. It helps to calm them down and eliminate nervous tension.

could liken it to a moving tingle. Again, we don't know why it occurs when and where it does. The pressure, or breeze effect, is often associated with a temperature feeling. Outside the pyramid, at the tip, for example, it is usually like a rising stream. Inside the pyramid, with the palm held upward, the sense of pressure is usually felt downward. The pressure is very slight, just like that which a gentle breeze might cause. I emphasize that these are body reactions which may or may not have anything to do with real movement.

## Is it true that the pyramid can heal?

This is one of the most important questions in the book. My answer is no. *However*, I also state that it does seem to aid the healing process by supplying additional energy so that the body can heal itself more quickly and effectively. The difference is subtle, but vital. The pyramid is not a magical panacea for all ills. Unless a person has the desire to be healed, the pyramid is not going to help much. This does not mean that the person has to believe in the power of the pyramid at all. It only means that the person has to be relatively free of any subconscious desire not to be healed. That is why the most successful healing results with the pyramid have been with minor ailments.

The pyramid has probably been used for headaches more than for any other complaint so far. According to my reading, the majority of headaches are caused by tension, and one thing that pyramid energy appears to do is to relax the muscles of the body. How it does this is a theoretical question right now, but if you accept the idea of an energy flow system in the body, it could do this by stimulating the natural flow, which would produce expansion and balance and thereby ease tension. At any rate, the headache results are so good that Drbal has applied for a patent on a pyramid-shaped cap specifically for headache relief. If you want to try this for yourself, at your own risk, of course, just pop a 6-inch-high cardboard pyramid on your head (when no one is around to laugh) and make sure that one side is facing north. You can use a larger-size pyramid, too, if you have one. Sometimes headaches disappear immediately and sometimes after an hour or more, apparently depending on the degree of tension involved. Interestingly, the effect of the pyramid appears to continue even after leaving it. That is, there are frequent reports of no headache relief while in the pyramid for a short time, but of the headache disappearing within half an hour or so after using it.

## What other minor ailments are helped with the pyramid?

My family and friends have used pyramids for several years as first aid for cuts and bruises. Remarkably, when a pyramid is placed over the hurt area, pain is almost instantly reduced or taken away entirely. I think this may be due to an expansive effect of the energy, for there is a relation between pain and tension. By observation it seems that the blood coagulates faster and that minor wounds heal more quickly, too. As for bruises, it is often noted that discoloration is lessened, particularly the "yellow" stage, and that they don't last as long as they do without treatment. We also get good results with stomachaches.

In fact, aches and pains of any kind seem to respond, at least in some degree, to treatment with a pyramid. People have even reported to me that they got temporary relief from arthritis, and the elimination of back pain is very common. Swelling is quickly eased and reduced, too, though I don't understand the process. To cite a personal case, my mother had a hard, painful lump on her hand for years before she began regular, daily treatments with a small, open-frame pyramid. Pain was reduced right away, though it would sometimes return between treatments. Most significant was that within three months the lump had virtually disappeared.

Pain relief occurs so frequently and consistently with a pyramid that my researchers and I almost take it for granted now. But, as I mentioned before, the pyramid does not heal—it only seems to add energy to the body. Pain relief is a convenience, but it does not mean that the problem has been resolved. Whatever caused the pain still has to be checked and treated in the way most suitable for it. Theoretically, the pyramid could reduce or eliminate the pain from a broken bone, but that doesn't mean it will reset the bone.

## Does the pyramid do anything for infections?

Based on the experience of my family and the reports I get, I'd say that pyramid energy tends to inhibit infections, including that of the common cold. In my house, colds have been extremely rare for several years, and when they do occur they rarely last more than a day. And flu is unheard-of. I believe this is partly due to good mental attitudes and partly to our regular use of the energy. Yet, volunteer subjects report that colds, sinus congestion, and insect bites clear up rapidly after treatment with a pyramid. An outstanding question is whether the energy from the pyramid actually slows down or stops the activity of infectious bacteria, or whether it is simply a case of giving the body more strength to fight off the infection itself. As yet, no one knows, but there are good arguments for both sides.

### What about more serious diseases, like cancer?

It would be wonderful to say—and prove—that in the pyramid we have at last found a cure for cancer. Unfortunately, that isn't the case. I personally do not think it will ever be the case, because I am of the strong opinion that cancer is caused by a bioenergetic distortion brought on by mental/emotional stress. However, that's only my opinion. Nevertheless, I do believe that in time it may be possible to use pyramids to relieve the pain associated with some forms of cancer and to relieve the stress that is (read *may be*, if you like) at the root of it. What the pyramid alone can never do is change a person's mental habits, which affect the emotions, which in turn affect the body.

### Do you see the possibility of pyramid hospitals in the near future?

I think that would be a mistake at this early stage in the research. There are still too many unknowns involved. For one thing, not everyone reacts favorably to the same amounts of pyramid energy. I will cover this point more fully toward the end of the chapter. Still, it is reasonable to predict that there may be special rooms or areas utilizing the pyramid form in hospitals not too long from now.

## Can pyramid water be used for treatment of cuts, colds, etc.?

In our experience, pyramid water is as effective as a pyramid, and in some cases it might be easier to use. It can be drunk or used to wash or swab the areas being treated.

## What do doctors say about all this?

As far as I know, there have been no official pronouncements, but you can bet your boots that the response from the majority would be negative at this point. I know of some chiropractors and a few dentists who are using pyramids or pyramid water as part of their overall treatment methods, but then they are usually more open-minded than medical doctors. What the researchers in this field would like to see is some honest medical research done on pyramid energy. I am confident that that will come about one of these days. The problem at present is finding enough MDs brave enough to face the wrath or ridicule of their colleagues.

## Is the pyramid an aphrodisiac? Does it increase the sex drive?

To hear some of the reports I get, you would think so! I have heard claims ranging from cure of impotence (inability to get an erection) to its being a fantastically stimulating environment for

the sex act. From the number of reports it is clear
that something is happening. My three hundred
mistresses and I (sorry, wife, just fooling!) speculate that these claims are based on the pyramid's
apparent amplification of body energy, which
would naturally affect sexual energy as well. Also,
the general relaxing effect of pyramid energy probably plays a role in reducing tension that might
be blocking full enjoyment of sex. To answer the
question of whether it is an aphrodisiac: In the
narrow sense of directly increasing sexual desire,
I have to say no; in the broader sense of affecting
sexual desire, I'd say yes.

*What effects, if any,*
*does the pyramid have on sleep?*

The reports from the field generally indicate
that sleeping regularly under a pyramid results
in a greater sense of well-being, more restful sleep,
fewer hours of sleep required, and a greater ability
to handle emotional stress. Since I have worked
daily for a number of years among many types of
pyramids and other energy devices I have never
until recently felt any urge to sleep under one.
But in preparation for this book my wife and I
undertook that kind of experiment. Her reaction
the first night was of a light, but very restful,
sleep. I, too, felt rested without the sensation of
ever having drifted into a deep sleep. Over a
period of two months we can both report more
restful sleep than ever, with varying degrees of
light or deep sleep on different days according
to our subjective sensations. We also seem to have
a consistently higher level of energy in spite of
the fact that we usually work a 16- to 18-hour

day. Some nights we sleep a full 8 hours and other times only 5 or 6, so that part isn't consistent. But even when we sleep less, we still feel just as energetic. Now we *like* sleeping under the pyramid and intend to continue.

## Does sleeping under a pyramid affect dreams?

For someone unused to the energy, dreams are often more vivid and easier to recall for the first few nights. I think this is because of the increased energy input which relaxes subconscious blocks that may have been built up against full dream recall. People also report often that they begin to dream in color for the first time. More than likely, they are merely recalling in color for the first time.

## Do you think everyone ought to sleep under a pyramid?

No, I wouldn't make such a sweeping recommendation. There are people who find that they cannot sleep at all under a pyramid. This is a temporary condition, as they would find if they kept at it. But it may upset them so much that they would be better off not continuing until they feel more sure of themselves. Once in a while, a person will find that sleeping under a pyramid gives him a headache. This is a case of overdose, and will be covered at the end of the chapter.

## Is the pyramid good for meditation?

Excellent, I'd say, because it aids relaxation while increasing psychic energy (or prana or mana or prime energy. There are different names for it in various system of thought). There are many forms of meditation, and the pyramid seems to enhance them all. Even reading can be a form of meditation, and many subjects report a greater ability to concentrate while studying under a pyramid. The ability to concentrate is a prime factor in deeper forms of meditation, too, and experienced meditators frequently give the pyramid glowing reports on this account.

## *Does it increase alpha production?*

Well, that's hard to say. Alpha brain waves are associated with some forms of meditation, but it is important to know that they are an effect of a certain mental state and not a cause. Consistent production of alpha waves—that is, consistent production of a mental state which produces alpha—requires a certain amount of training. The pyramid may aid in the maintenance of that state, but does not directly increase the amount of alpha produced. Some preliminary investigations tend to support the idea that experienced meditators can generate more alpha while under a pyramid, but the effects of suggestion are not entirely eliminated. For instance, researchers Kerrell and Goggin reported an experiment in which meditators were blindfolded while attached to a machine that monitors brain waves. A pyramid was lowered over them and raised without their conscious knowledge, and the results seemed to confirm a significant difference in brain wave patterns while within the pyramid. Kerrell and Goggin are properly cautious about the results, and I would add that it is highly probable that the *subcon-*

*scious* is aware of the raising and lowering of the pyramid, even if the conscious mind is not. Except for general relaxation, the pyramid does not bring about a particular state of consciousness, but instead serves to enhance the state one is trying to achieve. In any case, if you are looking for instant satori in a pyramid, you are in for a disappointment. The pyramid can give you certain experiences, but enlightenment is not one of them.

### Will the pyramid help to develop psychic abilities?

Here is where I have to give another yes-and-no answer. It depends so much on your understanding of what psychic development is. No, the pyramid will not suddenly turn you into a psychic. You will not become automatically telepathic, clairvoyant, or prophetic just by sitting under a pyramid. In other words, use of the pyramid will not *give* you psychic abilities. This is because you already have psychic abilities. They are latent in every human being, and active far more often than is realized.

What the pyramid will do is to help overcome any blocks you might have toward the realization of your innate abilities. Then it will help to intensify those abilities, much as the intake of carbohydrates will help to intensify the abilities of an athlete. So it would be fair to say that the pyramid can aid psychic development. It does this by increasing the amount of energy you have available.

### Can you be more specific?

All psychic phenomena require an expenditure of energy, including ordinary thought and imagi-

nation. We can call this bioenergy, and as far as
my staff and I can determine, the energy concentrated in the pyramid is identical to it. I have
already said that the pyramid enhances the state
of mind one is trying to achieve. As any number
of good books on parapsychology can tell you,
what we loosely call ESP works best in "non-
ordinary" states of mind. One of the keys to
attaining such states is relaxation, which the pyramid promotes. Beyond that, it actually seems to
give you the additional energy to carry out psychic
feats, depending on which type you are concen-
trating on.

For instance, we have found that the accuracy
of telepathic sending and receiving is increased
when one or both parties are in a pyramid. And
the several forms of clairvoyance are intensified,
too. One form is equated with visually seeing the
bioenergy field around people, what is frequently
called the "aura." This becomes easier to see
around a person who has charged himself up in
a pyramid, and it is easier for the viewer who has
been charged to see auras around others, whether
they have been in a pyramid or not. Another form
of clairvoyance is the reception of visual images.
Those who practice this report more sharply defined images and more vivid color. Of course, the
problem of interpretation is another matter. This
follows what I said before about the pyramid
giving experience but not enlightenment. Closely
related to the second type of clairvoyance is a
third form, often called "psychometry." It consists
of receiving images, impressions, and ideas from
an object held in the hand. Again, results are better
when it is done within a pyramid.

Just recently, a colleague of mine, Dr. Lawrence

Kennedy, told me of amazing psychokinetic results he is getting using a 4-foot-high equilateral-frame pyramid I built for him. (Psychokinesis is defined as "mind over matter".) Dr. Kennedy is the father of Chris Kennedy, who has been written about in a number of papers, including the *National Enquirer*, for his ability to bend keys and other objects with his mind. I have watched Chris operate from less than 3 feet away and attest to the validity of what this bright 14-year-old is doing. He told me that just before the bending occurs he feels a tremendous surge of energy going through him, which he then directs with his will. This confirms what I have previously said about psychic phenomena requiring energy. Chris now operates in a pyramid when he feels the need for extra energy.

Dr. Kennedy also bends objects, but in a slightly different way. He holds them, and when he feels the surge of energy he exerts a slight pressure and twists them into all sorts of "impossible" shapes. Inspired by him and his son I have done the same thing. During the process, the object, usually a spoon or a fork, seems to "soften" momentarily and becomes easy to bend. Then it hardens up and can't be moved until another surge of energy makes it "soft" again. Without the energy surge no one could bend it in the same way with the hands alone.

Another amazing thing is that Dr. Kennedy is now teaching others to generate the energy, allow it to flow through, and do the bending. He has told me that the success of his students increased dramatically when they attempted the bending in my pyramid. So far he has graduated fifteen successful "spoonbenders" from his psychic develop-

ment classes. Among these are the astounded dean
of a Western university and a housewife who has
accomplished the unusual feat of stretching the
bowl of a spoon until it has become as thin as
tinfoil.

Spoon and key bending only serve to demonstrate that we all have the ability to tap into
tremendous forces that can be used for more
beneficial purposes. One of these is healing, particularly in the form known as the laying on of
hands, or spiritual healing. This, too, is an ability
that everyone has, and I have personally taught
dozens of people to do it. When the pyramid is
used to amplify one's natural energy, the results
can become spectacular. Dr. Kennedy and Chris
are using the pyramid to aid in this work, as are
my staff and many other pyramid researchers
around the world. This, I believe, offers one of
the greatest potentials for pyramid use. Not only
can we use the energy to heal ourselves, but we
can transfer that energy from ourselves to others.

## What is the best way to use a pyramid for personal development?

Basically, there are four ways to use a pyramid.
You can sit or sleep inside one, you can suspend
one over a designated area, you can wear one on
your head, or you can put it under something.
What you do depends on time, space, and purpose. As an example, a pyramid built on the
Cheops model takes up more and more floor space
the higher you make it. A model 4 feet high has
a base that is 6 feet on a side. It is big enough to
sit in yoga-style, but not on a chair. It is big
enough to lie down in, however. Some people will

place such a model on their bed and hope it doesn't fall off as they move around during the night. A pyramid large enough to fit right over a bed could require a 12-foot base, more space than many of us can spare in a bedroom. Some people have therefore placed one or more pyramids under their beds, which is fine if there is enough room for them. Personally, I prefer a suspended pyramid for working and sleeping areas. They are always there when you want them and are conveniently out of the way. Over my bed I have a 6-inch-high cardboard pyramid which gives me very satisfactory results. Before our ceilings were changed, it was suspended by a string taped to the ceiling, but now it is suspended out from the wall. In the chapter on building your own pyramids I will show an easy way to do this. Over the desk I am working at right now I have a 3-foot-base openframe pyramid suspended from the crosspieces of an acoustical tile ceiling. It works beautifully.

Suspended pyramids are good as long as you don't want to move them around. Large free-standing pyramids fall into the same category, naturally. If you like to meditate or get charged up in your yard when the weather is good, or if you like to take a pyramid with you on an outing to the mountains, beach, or wherever, then the two choices are a pyramid cap or an easily disassembled freestanding model that isn't too large to tote around. The pyramid cap is ultra-convenient, especially if it is a cardboard model that folds flat or a framework that comes apart. The only problem is that if there are other people around, you may have to put up with curious stares or snickers. Probably the best freestanding model for carrying around is one 4 feet high with a 6-foot base. Those

6-foot-base lengths sound a little awkward, I know, but if the height were any less you'd be cramped, and this size is great for two people to stretch out under. There is a way to assemble shorter lengths into this size pyramid which I will tell you about in the chapter on building your own.

### Doesn't it matter about the focal point?

For certain meditation purposes, yes, but for other personal uses, no. Remember that there is energy concentrated all through the inside of the pyramid, around the outside, below it, and above the tip. In a meditative position inside a 4-foot model the focal point is approximately at the level of the solar plexus, depending on the size of the meditator. Apart from the King's Chamber area, the pyramid energy also seems to be more highly concentrated just below the apex. This is about where your head would be in a meditative position. If you are into astral travel, kundalini yoga, or seeking inspiration, then you would want to take full advantage of these concentration centers.

### Is a pyramid tent any better than an open frame for personal use?

Well, that depends on the weather and what you intend to do inside one. Seriously, I find no significant difference unless the sides are layered with metallic and organic materials, or unless the sides are all copper. Then the effects are greatly increased. But if the sides are simply made of wood, plastic, or cloth, then the only advantage is privacy.

*Then the materials used in a
pyramid do make a difference?*

No doubt about it, when they are used for
people (we have no data yet on pets). Copper
produces the strongest reactions of any other single
material. Wood evokes the most comfortable responses. Many of my subjects report that the
energy in a wood-frame pyramid somehow feels
"softer" than that of metal pyramids. There may
be psychological preference at work here, but
maybe not. Plastic usually feels more "active"
than other materials, and many people prefer steel
to aluminum. One pyramid manufacturer switched
over to higher-priced steel tubing for that reason.
On the other hand, some find aluminum delightful.
I don't think this is all psychological. Rather, I
believe that individuals can detect subtle differences in the energy given off by various materials and that their biological energy field is
complemented by some and repelled by others.
So far, it is copper and aluminum that provoke
the most varied responses in people.

## TROUBLESHOOTING

All is not roses in pyramidland. In response to
a question above I briefly mentioned overdose.
This is a problem that has not yet been sufficiently
recognized by researchers. If you recall, it is also
a problem with plants. It is possible to get too
much pyramid energy, with negative effects that
increase in seriousness as the dosage increases.
What makes the problem more complicated is
this: what is an overdose for one person may not

even be noticed by another. It is a very individual thing. This is why I would not recommend that whole hospitals be built in the form of pyramids or that everyone sleep under one. There is no way yet to predetermine who will be affected in what manner.

The symptoms of overdose follow a clearly defined pattern. First, there is a feeling of stuffiness, a feeling that one has had enough of the energy and would like to get away from it. If one remains within the field there may follow a slight headache which gets steadily worse until it is accompanied by a feeling of nausea. If the person persists in staying within the field, the above may be followed by aches or pains in the locations of old disorders. This will happen only in a very strong field such as that produced by a many-layered pyramid, or a very large one. Now, curiously, if a person hangs on in spite of all that, there follows a kind of "breakthrough" in which all the previous symptoms disappear and one begins to feel tremendous. It can be a painful place to reach, though, and it is quite unnecessary to go through it all, at least if one has the choice of leaving the pyramid at will.

The reasons why this happens are involved, but they have to do with the flow of energy in the body. Two persons may be equally sensitive to the energy in the sense of being able to feel it readily, but one may get adverse symptoms and the other may not. It rarely happens that a person gets a headache with plain 4-foot models or smaller, but it does happen occasionally and you should know about it. The solution is to either forgo the use of one until you are ready to try again, or to spend shorter times in the pyramid until you can comfortably take a longer dose. Our experience is that the more often you use a pyramid, regardless of the time period, the longer you are able to stay within it comfortably and the more able one is to handle more intense fields. Most of the subjects we have tested enjoy sleeping all night under a pyramid. It is only a few who experience discomfort.

Another phenomenon is the tendency to get very drowsy after spending a short time—say half an hour—in a pyramid and to have a great desire to take a nap. If you do nap, you generally feel very refreshed and full of vigor. The reasons for this are still obscure.

One of the common misconceptions people have is that if a little bit of something is good for you, then a whole lot must be better. On the contrary, a whole lot might just be dangerous. Ask the person who takes an overdose of drugs that are beneficial in small amounts. When some novice researchers hear that layered pyramids give off a more intense energy field, they sometimes overdo it. Be careful when creating highly concentrated fields of pyramid energy, even for laboratory research. It can hurt!

If you try pyramids and neither feel a thing nor get any reactions, don't despair and don't think it's all a hoax. You have a lot of company. In some people, sensitivity to the energy and its effects takes time to develop. It doesn't make you inferior or superior to anyone else. It's just your individuality.

Final question for this chapter:

*Is it necessary to believe in
the pyramid for it to work?*

I love that question. It pops up all the time. I
could say that from one point of view it is necessary for you to believe in the universe in order
for it to exist for you, but that's getting a bit philo-
sophical. What I usually say is, "Ask your plant,
your pet, or your razor blade." The pyramid works
whether or not you believe in it. Of course, belief
can enhance your reactions to the energy. Where
would psychosomatic medicine be without belief?
But your experiences with pyramids will be more
fruitful if you simply keep an open mind.

# Chapter 7

# PYRAMIDS AND
# NON-ORGANIC EFFECTS

In this chapter we go into effects that are far less subjective. To be covered are such things as the pyramid in relation to sharpening effects, removal or prevention of tarnish, strange effects on clocks, gems, and motors, and magnetism.

*Does the pyramid really sharpen razor blades?*

If it doesn't, it's doing a darn good imitation! Actually, there's a technical debate about whether the pyramid resharpens the blade, maintains its sharpness, or merely speeds up a natural process. There is no debate among users and researchers that effective blade life can be increased up to fifty times. That means some people who normally get only 5 good shaves from a blade have reported getting up to 250 shaves with the same type of blade when using a pyramid. Of course, the number of shaves any individual gets depends on factors like density of beard growth, type of lather used, orientation of the blade, etc. Overall, I find that 25 to 50 shaves is average using a Gillette Blue Blade in a 6-inch-high cardboard pyramid. This is based on worldwide reports and hundreds of tests by many researchers.

## How does it sharpen them?

Karl Drbal, the Czech researcher, says the pyramid maintains sharpness. He is of the opinion that the effect is caused by a regenerative action on the crystalline edge of the blade brought about by microwave dehydration. A razor blade will normally regenerate itself, that is, become sharper, after use just by being left alone for 2 weeks to a month. You can prove that by trying it yourself. What the pyramid appears to do is to speed up this natural process so that it takes place in 24 hours. Along with the regeneration of the edge, the dehydration effect (or accelerated evaporation, if you prefer) strengthens the steel of the blade itself. A Dr. Carl Benedicks of Stockholm has found that steel can suffer a loss of firmness of up to 22 percent through being impregnated with water molecules. The regeneration takes place only for a blade receive normal wear through shaving. If the blade were chipped, for instance, the pyramid wouldn't make the blade fill itself in. This microwave dehydration theory is what enabled Drbal to obtain his patent from the Czech government, after ten years of testing to see whether a blade was really resharpened. The theory is still a theory with a lot of holes, but no one has come up with a better one yet in relation to razor blades.

## Why doesn't the blade keep on sharpening without limits?

No one knows the answer to that, but I have an idea based on my own experience. I find that the blade resharpens, all right, but not quite right back up to its original pristine newness. Instead of pulling and scratching the way a non-treated blade does when it wears out, however, a treated blade just gradually stops cutting until it runs smoothly over your face. I think this is because the actual material of the blade has been worn away so that even if the edge is regenerated, it becomes rounded.

## Do you always get smooth shaves right up until the blade wears out?

No, not always. There is a strange effect that occurs along about the twenty-fifth shave or so. What happens is that the blade suddenly gives a very poor shave for one or two days, and then gives excellent shaves after that. Drbal experienced this and thought it might be due to meteorological or cosmic disturbances. My own observations suggest tend to show the moon as the culprit, but this is a long way from being proved. Nevertheless, I wouldn't be surprised if we find that the moon's gravitational pull affects the magnetic field of the earth, which in turn affects the operation of the pyramid, which then affects the sharpening of the razor blade. Anyway, if your blade seems to give out before you think it should, give it a chance. Wait a day or so and try again. The blade will likely be back up to par.

## Will the pyramid sharpen a blade that's already dull?

Yes, though it won't do it in 24 hours. Reports show that it takes anywhere from 3 weeks to a couple of months for a dull blade to show improvement under a pyramid.

## Where do you put the blade in the pyramid?

The best place to put the blade is on a platform at the "phi point" or King's Chamber area, or one third of the distance up from the center of the base to the tip. It doesn't matter whether you make the platform out of the same material as the pyramid. For a 6-inch-high pyramid I find that the cap from a can of spray deodorant does quite well as a platform.

## Does it matter how you put the blade on the platform?

Yes, the positioning of the blade makes a great deal of difference in the results you will get. For reasons that still aren't clear, the sharpening effect is better when the blade edges are facing each and west or, to put it another way, when the long axis of the blade is in line with magnetic north. Naturally, your pyramid will also be lined up with one face toward north, so both the blade and the pyramid are interacting with the magnetic field of the earth. The blade will sharpen when laid in a different direction, but not as well and not for as long a time.

### *Is it necessary to lay the blade flat?*

No, it isn't. As a matter of fact, I was pleased to find that I could get just as good results by leaving the blade in the razor, as long as the alignment was correct. This means the handle of the razor would be pointing east or west, and the blade would be tilted.

### *Does the size of the pyramid make any difference?*

Not as far as I can tell, and I haven't seen any reports that claim faster results with a larger pyramid. The pyramid first used by Drbal was about 8 inches high, but he later found that he could regularly get about a hundred shaves with a cardboard or styrene model only 3 inches high. Of course, with this model you'd have to take the blade out of the razor. Before you ask, I'll also say that the material the pyramid is made out of doesn't really seem to make a difference, either, as far as bladesharpening goes.

### *Will the pyramid sharpen anything besides razor blades?*

It sure will. Tony Sassoon, the hairdresser, uses them to keep his scissors sharp, and many people use them to keep knives sharp. I have an X-acto knife that I have used in my business for 3 years without needing to change the blade and it has made thousands of cuts mostly through heavy-gauge posterboard. All I do is leave it under a pyramid between uses. An important factor in this is the sharpness of the blade to begin with. The sharper the blade when you start out, the longer it will give good service with treatment.

## How does the pyramid remove tarnish?

It would probably be better to say that it loosens it. A couple of years ago I heard excited reports that the pyramid would remove tarnish from a silver coin and leave it in neat little piles all around it. That was too much even for *me* to believe. In testing I found that those reports were highly exaggerated, but the results were fascinating nonetheless. I used a silver 1964 Kennedy half-dollar at the phi point in a 6-inch-high clear styrene pyramid (I wanted to see who was going to make those neat little piles). The coin was pretty badly tarnished when I put it inside. After 3 days it didn't look any different, so I took it out and happened to run my thumb across the face of the coin. My skin was black. I rubbed some more and discovered that the tarnish was easily removed from all the high-relief areas of the coin. I used a cloth to get at the lower areas, but that tarnish didn't come off. So then I left the coin in the pyramid for 3 weeks, hoping to loosen all of it. It was a disappointment because there was no improvement. Apparently everything that could be done to the tarnish was done in those first three days. Thinking the oil in my skin might have had something to do with it (always remember those variables!) I repeated the experiment with another coin, being careful to handle it only with a cloth. I got the same results. Similar effects were achieved with copper and steel.

### And it will prevent tarnish, too?

Let's be conservative and change that to "retard." Tarnishable items don't tarnish as fast when they are kept under a pyramid. This holds true for silverware, copper items, and iron or steel. I haven't tried it with anything else.

### Why does this happen?

Beats me. That ever-present dehydration effect may have something to do with it. Tarnish is a result of oxidation, and oxidation takes place more rapidly in moist air. If the pyramid is creating an environment in which the air is less moist, then that may be the reason for the slowdown in oxidation. Unfortunately, that doesn't seem to explain the loosening effect of tarnish already present. I suspect the latter is an electromagnetic reaction, but I don't pretend to be able to explain it.

### Can't this have other practical applications?

Offhand I can see that it ought to lessen the maintenance problems of certain electrical devices that depend on good contact between parts. If tarnishing is retarded, then electrical contact should remain effective for a longer period of time.

This effect is presently being used in another way, too. Or at least it's the only explanation I have for some far-out-sounding reports. I can't vouch for them, but the people involved swear that it happens. What I'm talking about is the use of pyramids to maintain efficient operation of vehicle motors.

## What?

That's what I said the first time I heard it. There are quite a few people who claim that pyramids make their cars run better. One man is supposed to have suspended a pyramid from his garage rafters so his car could get "charged" overnight. According to the report, he never had to change the oil or filter and needed no major repairs for 156,000 miles of driving. He did add oil to the motor, transmission, and rear end as necessary. The idea is that the pyramid energy acts to reduce friction on the moving parts. Whether this story is any more valid than the one about the tarnish being set out in little piles, I don't know. But a good friend of mine who is a truck driver keeps a pyramid in his cab over the engine and is convinced that it helps. There are claims that electric motors run smoother and longer under a pyramid as well. All I can say is try it.

## What about the clock mystery?

It's a mystery, that's for sure. As near as I can determine, the first person to experience it was a man from California who wrote of it to Bill Cox, an avid researcher and editor of *The Pyramid Guide*. It seems the man had made a cardboard pyramid and placed it on his desk over a small folding clock from Germany of the type that is used for traveling. Apparently the clock hadn't been running for 7 or 8 years because it had been wound too tight. After a few days the man decided to take the clock to the jeweler. I took it from underneath the pyramid and when he opened it, he was surprised to find that the hands had moved from the position he knew they had been at, and in addition the clock was completely run down. He rewound it and put it back under the pyramid, leaving it overnight. In the morning it had run down again and the hands were at a position one and a half hours different from the previous night. There was no way to tell whether it had run that length of time or for a little over 24 hours. It isn't clear from the report, but apparently that much time at least must have elapsed since he had last checked it. Although he rewound it, the clock would not function. The third time he tried it, it did the same thing. The clock ran down and the hands moved, but it still would not work when he wound it back up. The pyramid did not fix the clock, but it certainly did something to it.

Cox then tried a similar experiment under different conditions. The first time he set a foil-covered cardboard pyramid over a small windup clock and left it for 24 hours, but did not notice anything out of the ordinary. In this experiment he had placed the clock upright, so the next time he laid it on its back with the twelve position toward the north. After 24 hours the hands were where they should have been, but instead of requiring several turns to rewind, it only took two. It should be noted that Cox's clock was in good working order when he started.

I tried the experiment once on a watch that had been wound too tight. I left it under the pyramid for 24 hours and when I checked it the watch was still wound too tight, but the hands had moved! That upset me so much at the time that I didn't repeat it (a terrible way for a true researcher to act) and haven't taken the time since to do it again. However, a number of researchers with whom I am in contact say that their clocks and watches have done strange things when left under a pyramid. The results are not consistent. Sometimes the watches run down after having been wound too tight and work perfectly afterward. Sometimes the hands move more than they should. And sometimes nothing happens at all. I don't have any way of explaining this. Controlled testing is needed to make any sense out of it. It would be nice to have a report from a dedicated researcher who has put a too-tightly-wound clock under a clear pyramid and stayed up all night to watch the hands move.

*What is the relation of
gemstones or crystals to the pyramid?*

There are a number of relationships and different ways that crystals have been used in pyramid research. In some cases the interest is concentrated on similarity of form, in others in similarity of energy output. Experiments have been done with crystal growth, charging of crystals, and using crystals as amplifiers.

*What do you mean by similarity of form?*

The pyramid shape has often been likened to that of a crystal, but in reality it is only shaped like half a crystal of certain types. If you put two pyramids base to base you get an octahedron, an eight-sided geometrical figure. Researchers have been fascinated by the fact that this shape occurs as a natural crystal formation with a few materials.

Among these are gold, chromite, and fluorite. One line of research has been to test the double pyramid or octahedral shape as an energy generator, but so far the results have been mediocre. Another line is to test the energy generation of octahedral crystals. Fluorite is the easiest to obtain, but the results of my tests have been very disappointing. Perhaps the incompleteness of the pyramid form creates a dynamic interplay of forces which are canceled out or dampened when the form is completed as an octahedron. At least that sounds good, doesn't it? I would be interested in hearing from anyone who has had positive results with octahedrons. As another approach, research is presently going on to test the healing qualities of gold formed into pyramids. There are some health spas which report very beneficial results from covering people with gold-bearing sand, so there is reason to hope for a successful outcome to the experiments.

By the way, the theory of incomplete dynamics doesn't seem to apply to the tetrahedron, often described as a three-sided pyramid (four, actually, with the base). It is a complete geometrical form, and yet it has a very active energy field. However, to my knowledge there are no natural crystals with this shape.

### Do some crystals give off pyramid energy naturally?

They give off energy which seems to be the same as that of the pyramid, at any rate. I suspect all crystals do, but some do more than others. One of the best generators of this type, which I have tested extensively, is "ordinary" quartz. A scientist

by the name of Reichenbach demonstrated a polar-
ized flow of energy from natural quartz crystals
back in the 19th century. The properties of this
energy as he described them were similar to those
attributed to the pyramid today. As an example,
a quartz crystal held under or over, or used to stir,
a glass of water will charge it in a few minutes
the same way as the pyramid does. In a series of
tests I ran, virtually all of my subjects were able
to feel the flow of energy from the tip of a quartz
crystal, and the sensations they described were
identical to those felt with the pyramid. What I
find most interesting is that quartz is well known
and extensively used for its electrical properties:
When a crystal is twisted, it generates an electric
current. This was the basis for the old crystal
radio sets and is growing in use today. It is another example of the close relationship between
pyramid energy and electricity.

Quartz crystals have been used as amplifiers in
pyramids with interesting results. Since the pyramid gives off energy and the quartz gives off
energy, it stands to reason that if you put the
two of them together you should have an increase
in effects. This is exactly what seems to happen.
For this kind of work the crystal is usually placed
at the bottom of the pyramid or suspended from
the tip so that it is pointing downward toward
the King's Chamber.

A few people have gone to the trouble to cut
quartz into pyramid forms to see what effects are
produced. I have had a personal experience with
one such quartz pyramid made by Marcel Vogel,
a crystallographer in San Jose, California, better
known for his research into man-plant communica-
tion. Dr. Vogel uses quartz crystals as transmitter-

amplifiers of human thought. In one experiment we conducted he used a quartz pyramid about an inch high to transmit a beam of energy to me when I was twenty-five yards away. According to my subjective sensations, I felt the beam very strongly, just as if I were standing under a large enclosed pyramid.

## What effect does the pyramid have on crystal growth?

The results are uncertain as yet. You may know that it is possible to grow certain crystals at home in chemical solutions. There are some good kits on the market for this. A few early reports stated that the pyramid caused unusual crystal formations. You will find, however, that unusual formations sometimes appear even without a pyramid, though something other than a pyramid may be causing a similar energy reaction. What we need is—please don't get tired of reading this—controlled testing. Amazingly, no one has yet reported tests of crystal growing under a pyramid with a control.

## Why haven't you done all these controlled tests you say are needed?

Ah, that question had to pop up sometime. If this book nets me a million dollars, I promise I'll do that. In any field where experiments have to be done in a spare corner in one's spare time and the profusion of ideas is endless, some things will have to go undone unless a particular person takes an interest in them. Even when regular laboratories become available for this work—which is happening—there will be too many ideas for the facilities and time available. This is why I want to present as many ideas as possible to the general public. I hope that enough people will become interested so that someone will be doing each needed thing. If we sit back and wait for the other guy to do the work, then many aspects of this field will never be explored.

*Apart from alignment,*
*where does magnetism fit in?*

Would you be surprised to learn that magnets also give off what we can call pyramid energy? In the late 18th century magnets were used for healing and charging water by Anton Mesmer, who also accidentally discovered hypnotism (mesmerism). Reichenbach in the 19th century confirmed many of Mesmer's findings and added new discoveries. Within the past few years excellent work on biomagnetics (the relation of magnetism to the living system) has been carried out by Albert Roy Davis and Walter Rawls of Florida. A magnet can produce all the phenomena of a pyramid. As with the quartz crystals, I tested subjects with magnets and got the same sense responses as with a pyramid. As further objective proof, I will blow my own horn a bit. I was the first person to sharpen a razor blade with an orgone accumulator (up to 800 shaves with one device of my design) which showed a definite relationship between orgone and pyramid energy. At present I am doing the same thing with a magnet. Using a stainless blade which had already undergone 90 shaves by treatment with a layered device, I have now obtained 25 more shaves with the same blade using a magnet. I expect it to continue sharpening for a good while. This is also a first.

Magnets make better pyramid amplifiers than crystals because they seem to give off more energy. Please understand that I am not equating the pyramid energy with magnetism. There is an important relationship, but they are not the same thing. In a way, you could compare it to the relationship between electricity and magnetism. They are not the same thing, but a magnet in motion creates an electrical current and an electric current generates a magnetic field. So a magnet emits pyramid-type energy, but so do nonmagnetic materials.

*How do you use a magnet as a pyramid amplifier?*

The easiest way is to simply place the magnet somewhere in the base of the pyramid. It should definitely increase the number of shaves you get, but be careful with charging plants because it will be easy to give them an overdose. Ditto for people.

*Does the strength of the
magnet make a difference?*

Up to a certain point, but after that, biosystems no longer react. The exact field strength point at which this takes place is not clear, but I would direct you to the books of Rawls and Davis listed in the recommended bibliography at the end of this book.

*Haven't any magnetic effects been
noted with the pyramid itself?*

Yes, but they are pretty strange. I'll list a few here.

—Some researchers report that suspended pyramids, even cardboard ones, tend to orient themselves to magnetic north more often than not.

—One researcher has reported that a steel pyramid placed over a compass disorients the needle 38 degrees east, and when five such pyramids are stacked, the needle is disoriented 90 degrees east.

—Kerrell, who has been mentioned before, used a magnetic field analyzer on a 20-inch-base steel-frame pyramid and received fluctuating readings at different points along the base and the corners. This shouldn't have occurred, according to our present understanding of magnetism.

—A man who built a 14-inch-base sheet-steel pyramid found that when a compass was moved straight up from the base the needle reversed itself at a point two-thirds of the distance from the base to the apex.

Research is still going on in major universities. Accurate magnetic measurements take sophisticated equipment and I'm glad some scientists are finally becoming interested enough in pyramids to do it.

*What's a good "nonorganic" experiment?*

Assuming you are just getting into pyramid energy, the razor blade experiment is a good one to start with, if you shave, of course. By the way, a lot of women who shave their legs have done this experiment, too. For a comparison test that doesn't take too long, use something like a Gillette Blue Blade. Get a package of blades and use one as you normally would. When that one no longer shaves well (5 shaves is the limit for me), put that one aside and take another one, placing it under a pyramid as described above between shaves. Approximately 24 hours of treatment gives the best results. Keep a record, and if you note any dull cycles be sure to put down weather conditions or anything else you think might be responsible. "Trac II" blades will work, too. Stainless lasts a lot longer than the blue blades, so be patient if you use one. Some people also report good results with electric shaver heads. I haven't tried these, so you will have to find out for yourself how to orient them.

## TROUBLESHOOTING

Orientation is very important in blade-sharpening experiments, as is the alignment of the blades. Be sure to check these if results are less than desired. Also check to see that you aren't too close to large masses of steel or iron, which would mess up your compass readings. Drbal suggested that you also stay clear of electrical appliances. He was thinking of microwave interference, but I think the problem has more to do with the magnetic fields set up by electric current. In my experience this is only critical where close orientation is important. In water-charging or dehydration experiments I don't find it significant.

For any of the other nonorganic experiments

mentioned in this chapter you are pretty much
on your own, because not enough has been done
to determine troubleshooting procedures apart
from common sense. Think of it as a wide-open
area.

# Chapter 8

# PYRAMIDS AND
# ELECTRONICS

A constant dream of mankind has been a free energy source, or at least one that was extremely cheap. Wind power has provided this in some instances. Solar power, though expensive now, has possibilities of becoming much cheaper sometime in the future. Around the turn of the century, the electrical genius, Nicolas Tesla, made an abortive attempt to "electrify" the whole earth so that a man could stick a pole in the ground anywhere and supply his electrical needs.

Now with the pyramid there are voices saying that this is the energy source of the future, and all for free. Part of that is wishful thinking. By the time the pyramid, or a derivation thereof, is able to supply usable energy efficiently the system will most likely be in the hands of manufacturers and pyramid power companies who will charge well for supplying it. Ah well, someone has to

pay for the development, so they might as well
get something out of it. At any rate, don't expect
to power your appliances by setting a cardboard
pyramid on your roof. But there is a strong relationship between the pyramid energy and electricity, and the results even at this early stage
have been fascinating. Let's start out with what
appears to be a direct conversion of pyramid
energy to usable electricity—the charging of
batteries.

### Can pyramids really charge batteries?

There are an awful lot of people who think so.
Let me quote from a report by one of my researchers, which is typical of many I've received:
"I built a pyramid for my 11-year-old son and
told him of its powers, etc. A few weeks later I
was going to the market and asked him if he
needed any batteries for his tape recorder. He
told me that he probably wouldn't be needing any
for a while because he always put the old ones
under his pyramid and it recharged them. He had
figured this out for himself."

### Have any tests been run?

A report of such a test appeared in the January-
February 1974 issue of *The Pyramid Guide*. The
experimenter purchased two packs of "D" batteries
with two batteries to a pack, and then marked
one from each pack to make sure one set was not
older than the other. All four batteries were put
in a charger for 24 hours to bring them to a peak
charge. The unmarked batteries were placed on a
shelf and the marked pair were put inside a

pyramid (size not mentioned) for 1 week. Then both sets were put in flashlights and left on for 4 hours, when the lights became very dim. Next, both flashlights were turned off for 1 week. After that the "unmarked" flashlight would not light and the batteries turned out to have acid all over their exteriors. The "pyramidized" flashlight lit up with about 50 percent brightness.

Not yet satisfied, the researcher left the "pyramid" flashlight on for 1 hour a day for the next 5 days, during which the light became very weak. Then the flashlight was left (apparently off, but it is not stated) on a shelf for a month. No light was produced at this time. The batteries were treated in the pyramid for 24 hours and put back in the flashlight. The light was about 25 percent of normal and rapidly diminished to very dim in an hour. The batteries got another 48-hour charge and the light was again 25 percent normal, becoming very dim in 2 hours. Back to the pyramid went the batteries for a full week. On the last test the batteries gave out with "one big cameralike flash" and went permanently dead. According to his estimate, the untreated batteries produced light for a total of 4 hours, as compared to 12 hours for the treated batteries.

## Anything with stricter controls?

Glad you asked. Following is a report of a test I conducted. A "Manabox" is a device of mine which puts out the same type of energy, which I call *mana*, as the pyramid:

"Object: To test the recharging effect, if any, of mana on batteries. Procedure: Four size "C" Tosari brand flashlight batteries were purchased

and tested with a SANWA model U-50 DNC
Multimeter using a No. 44 lamp load. All four
produced 1.55 volts, and were numbered 1 through
4. They were shorted to the following voltages:

No. 1 = .2V
No. 2 = .1V
No. 3 = .3V
No. 4 = .2V

"The batteries were left standing overnight and
checked again the next morning in the same way.
They were then distributed as follows: No. 1 on
a forty-fold aluminum/plastic Manabox; No. 2 on
a one-fold copper/plastic Manabox; No. 3 in a
6"-high styrene pyramid; No. 4 as control. All
batteries were checked daily at approximately
9:30 A.M. for 1 week, then at weekly intervals for
2 weeks. On that date they were taken off the test
arrangements and checked again 24 hours later.
Results:

|  | No. 1 | No. 2 | No. 3 (pyramid) | No. 4 (control) |
|---|---|---|---|---|
| Day 1 (pretest) | .95V | .9V | .95V | .95V |
| Day 2 | 1V | 1V | 1V | 1V |
| Day 3 | 1.05V | 1V | 1.05V | 1V |
| Day 4 | 1.09V | 1.01V | 1.05V | 1.01V |
| Day 5 | 1.1V | 1.05V | 1.1V | 1.05V |
| Day 6 | 1.1V | 1.05V | 1.1V | 1.05V |
| Day 7 | 1.15V | 1.09V | 1.1V | 1.05V |
| Day 14 | 1.1V | 1.09V | 1.09V | 1.05V |
| Day 21 | 1.2V | 1.19V | .9V(?) | 1.1V(?) |
| Day 22 | No change in any of the batteries. | | | |

"Comments: Though the amounts are minimal, it's clear the test batteries definitely increased in voltage over the control during the first week. Even No. 2, which started out with .05 volts less than the others, exceeded the control by the seventh day. No. 1 made the most marked change, which suggests that the Manabox higher energy output must have been a factor.

"The drop of .05 volts in No. 1 in the second week is puzzling, as is the subsequent jump of .1 volts during the next week. So is the jump of .1 volts in No. 2 in the same week. Note that No. 4 also increased by .05 volts in that week after having appeared to be remaining steady at 1.05 for a week and a half. Relatively startling is the sudden drop in No. 3 to a point below the others after a steady climb.

"What caused the rises and drop in that last week? Test arrangements hadn't changed. Atmospheric conditions? The weather here was fairly stable. Sunspots? Radio reception seemed normal. Planetary energies? Venus went direct on Day 15 and Mercury went retrograde on Day 17. According to traditional astrology, a retrograde Mercury is supposed to affect our mental energy, and Mercury in mythology is the same as Hermes/Thoth, who supposedly had something to do with the pyramids. This may be farfetched, but in exploring an unknown we should consider everything."

It is too bad I wasn't conducting razor blade tests at the same time. It would have been interesting to see whether a decrease in blade sharpness would have coincided with the voltage drop in the pyramid-treated battery. I propose two tentative facts based on the above experiment. One, that pyramid energy is convertible to electrical energy; and two, that pyramid energy is subject to fluctuations. The causes for the latter remain unknown.

## Has anyone else shown such an electrical conversion?

Apart from those who regularly claim battery-charging results, the only other example I know of was reported by a West German reader of *The Pyramid Guide* in the November-December 1974 issue. I will quote the letter in full as it appeared:

"Some months ago in the *Bavarian Staatsbibliothek* I read an interesting article written by an Austrian (or German?) friend of Karl Drbal. He conducted the following experiment: A glass of water was placed under a pyramid model. Two electrodes of the *same* metal were immerged into the water. (Normally *same metal electrodes* produce no volts, as you know). An attached galvanometer got a weak response in spite of the same metals. Later he replaced the galvanometer by a curve-writer and got very interesting readings. I hope the periodical is not yet out of print. If interested you can order it from: Herold-Verlag, 8000 Munchen 71 (W. Germany). The mentioned periodical: *Zeitschrift für Radiesthesie* Nr. 2, April/June/Ausgabe 1973."

This experiment should be easy to reproduce if you have any electrical knowledge. Why don't you try it?

## If pyramids can affect mechanical motors, can they affect electrical appliances?

Intriguingly, the answer just may be affirmative.

Bill Cox, editor of the aforementioned *Pyramid Guide*, claims that a pyramid has helped maintain the smooth operation of his electric razor. I myself have used pyramid energy devices to improve radio and television reception and to bring back the lights on an electric digital display clock after they went out.

My use of the device for improving television reception was inspired by another report to *The Pyramid Guide* in the March-April 1973 issue. The researcher was getting very poor reception with a Zenith black-and-white portable TV. He had just made a 9-inch-high aluminum sheet pyramid, so he decided to see what would happen if he placed it on the set directly above the picture tube. At first there didn't seem to be any improvement, but the reception got better over a period of two weeks, and was very good at the end of three weeks. Thinking a change in the weather might have had something to do with it, he decided to experiment further with his color TV. He had very good reception on channels 2 and 4, poor reception on 5 and 13, and fair on the rest.

He used picture-frame wire to hang the pyramid above the set and over the picture tube. A portion of the same wire attached to the pyramid was connected to the lead-in on the back of the TV. A wire going to one side of the roof antenna was attached to the other lead-in. Channels 5 and 13, the ones he had been having trouble with, then came in very well, but 2 and 4, which had been best, now produced only black and white.

The pyramid was then disconnected and the roof antenna hooked up to both lead-ins. Now 2 and 4 were great and 5 and 13 were poor again.

None of the other channels were affected with either arrangement. The gentleman noted that, thanks to the pyramid, he had been able to watch the Thursday night fights in color for the first time in three years.

Next he tried two pyramids, one connected to each of the lead-ins, and with the roof antenna disconnected completely. This time all the channels came in strong, but the color wasn't steady and the picture was blurred. He ended by saying that he was going to try mounting the pyramids on the roof, and that he was going to make pyramid antennas by wrapping wire continuously around a framework.

## What are some other ways in which pyramids and electricity are related?

Well, you know from what has been said before that pyramid energy can be made to flow along a wire somewhat like electricity. A novel use of this effect, with many implications, is obtained by combining a pyramid, a coil, and a variable condenser. The first time I ran across this was at the E.S.P. Laboratory in Los Angeles, run by Al Manning. I don't know whether Manning invented the idea, but he sells such a set-up which he calls the "Atlantean Generator."

I have built my own versions of this combination, so I will give you a first-hand account of what it is like. Basically, a copper wire is attached to a pyramid of any type or material. It can be attached to the tip, or run along the base, or connected to the corners, I don't find any significant difference in the way it is attached. The other end of the wire is attached to a step-up induction

coil or transformer. For you out there without
any electrical background, use solid wire about
the thickness of telephone wire or the type found
in most electrical toys. Strangely enough, it doesn't
really matter whether it is insulated or not. Wrap
the free end of the wire from the pyramid about
60 times around a cardboard tube. The tube from
a roll of bathroom tissue will do nicely. Attach the
other end of the wire to the pyramid again. Then
take another wire and do 100 turns around the
tube in the opposite direction. You may need some
tape to hold the whole coil together. The second
wire will be on top of the first. Attach one free
end of the second wire to a variable condenser.
This is like the tuning knob on a radio. You should
be able to pick up a suitable one in a radio supply
store for a couple of dollars. Run another wire
from the condenser to a flat piece of aluminum
or copper, with one edge bent so that it can stand
up. Take the other free end of the second wire
and attach it to a similar piece of metal, and position the two flat pieces so they face each other
from 3 to 6 inches apart. (See Fig. 7.) Now you
have a Pyramid/Coil Combo.

*Fine, but what do I do with it?*

Everything you can do with the pyramid alone.
Each of the plates emanates an energy field, which
is intensified by having them face each other. So
you can set whatever it is you want to treat between them. However, there are two things about
this arrangement which made it particularly interesting. First of all, the induction coil actually
does amplify the energy from the pyramid when
the second coil has more turns than the first. By

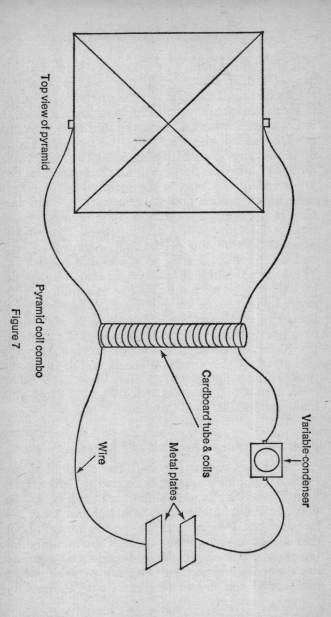

Top view of pyramid

Pyramid coil combo

Figure 7

Cardboard tube & coils

Variable condenser

Wire

Metal plates

radionic measurement,* there is no increase in energy output if both wires have the same number of turns. The second interesting thing is that the energy flow is modulated by the variable condenser. That is, the flow is lessened or strengthened by turning the dial. So, by introducing electrical elements we have produced additional electrical-type characteristics.

*Have you any idea how this happens?*

Some ideas. One of the early pyramid researchers, Verne Cameron, also found that coils gave off the same type of energy. My staff and I have since demonstrated this many times. The coil arrangement described above will give off energy of its own accord. You can test this by placing your hand near the open end of the tube around which the wires are wound. If you can feel the energy emanating off the tip of a pyramid, you should be able to feel the same sensations here. However, in this case, even two coils with the same number of turns ought to step up the energy output. This aspect needs more investigation.

As for the variable condenser, or capacitor, this is essentially an adjustable, multi-layer orgone plate. To give you a brief background, between the thirties and fifties of the century a scientist named Wilhelm Reich developed a device made of alternating layers of metallic and organic material which apparently collected or accumulated an energy he called "orgone." I have since proved that orgone is identical to pyramid energy (on

*Radionics is a form of dowsing or radiesthesia that uses various machines, devices and apparatus to obtain precise measurements.

my writing schedule is a book about our experiments with orgone devices and their refinements). The similarity of a layered orgone device to an electrical capacitor/condenser intrigued me to the point where, through experimentation, I found that even these common electrical units accumulate and radiate a pyramid-type energy field, whether they are hooked up to electric current or not. One of the factors in orgone output with layered devices is plate area—in fact, they seem to follow all the rules of capacitance. A variable condenser varies the amount of layered plate area and thus, assuming my theories are correct, the amount of orgone energy output. If you make the pyramid/coil combo described in this chapter, you should be able to feel a difference in the energy between the two end plates as you turn the knob of the condenser.

## *How about practical applications?*

One that comes to mind immediately is with plant experimentation. You remember that we said some plants are supersensitive to pyramid energy. With the PCC (pyramid/coil combination) you can vary the amount of energy directed to the plant by adjusting the condenser and the distance between the end plates. If you can get a condenser with dial settings you can introduce some accuracy to the process. If you know how to use a pendulum you can quickly arrive at the proper energy adjustment for a particular plant. I am sure you will think of other applications as well.

### Are there any other electrical correspondences?

Another area that provides a lot of food for thought is static electricity. Wherever you have a static electric field you have some pyramid energy effects, but not necessarily vice versa. So pyramid energy is not the same as static electricity, as some have tried to say, but there is an intimate connection. It is my expectation that through a study of pyramid energy we are going to learn much more about electromagnetism.

To give you an idea of how close the correspondence is, you may have heard of something called a "pyramid energy plate." It is a piece of aluminum, usually anodized (coated), that gives off an energy field exactly like the pyramid. It can be used to sharpen blades, treat water, etc. It differs from a pyramid, however, in that the charge of energy eventually wears off unless the plate is recharged. This can be done by leaving it in a pyramid or on a pyramid grid. The thing to note is that the plate is originally charged by zapping it with 100,000 volts of static electricity. This means that both the static electricity and the pyramid are doing the same thing to the plate.

You can experiment with this for yourself if you have access to an electrostatic generator or a Tesla coil. For some of my simple experiments I just charged a piece of tooling copper about 2 inches square that I got from a hobby shop with 50,000 volts for 1 minute, and compared it with an uncharged piece of the same copper. Try it for mellowing coffee or sharpening a razor blade. It works!

*What is another experiment a beginner
can do in relation to pyramids and electricity?*

I suggest a test on the recharging of batteries.
Get two cheap flashlights of the same kind, small
enough to fit under at least a 9- to 10-inch-base
pyramid (6 inches high). Try to get a battery
package with four batteries in it, if you can. If
not, do your best to get batteries that seem the
same age. Or you can mix batteries from two
packages for an equal distribution. Put the batteries in the flashlights and leave one flashlight
(always the same one, of course) under a pyramid
overnight and the other on a shelf well away from
the first. The next day, and for every day thereafter until the experiment is ended, allow both
flashlights to remain on for 2 hours. Then replace
them in their respective storage areas. Keep notes
of the comparative apparent brightness of each
as well as any other factors you notice as you go
along. End the experiment when one of the flashlights no longer lights. You should learn something about pyramids charging batteries from this,
although I remind you to be wary of drawing
absolute conclusions from one experiment.

## TROUBLESHOOTING

Aside from common sense and what has gone
before, there are no particular troubleshooting
points for this area.

# Chapter 9

# THE PYRAMID AS A
# WISH MACHINE

This chapter might seem pretty far out to most of you. From the traditional point of view of physics it is very unscientific (much more so than what has been said so far), but in terms of the new sciences of parapsychology and paraphysics it is quite valid. Regardless, no study of pyramid energy would be complete without a discussion of this aspect.

*What do you mean by a "wish machine"?*

I mean that virtually ever since the discovery that the pyramid is an energy source, it has been used to try to make dreams or wishes come true. The pyramid has long been a symbol of occult wisdom and power, and there is a strong under-current of belief in magic in Western society, very

thinly overlaid with scientific rationalism. That's
one reason so many advertisers use the word
"magic" in their sales pitches.

### But isn't this just superstition?

In regard to the pyramid, I have to say ambigu-
ously yes and no. Yes, it is superstition to believe
that the pyramid, or pyramid energy, can bring
about changes in conditions and circumstances *by
itself*. No, it is not superstition when one uses the
pyramid in conjunction with certain principles of
creating changes in experience, even if this is
done unconsciously, as it usually is.

### Are you saying that it will work if you believe in it?

Not quite, although such a belief will certainly
strengthen the effects. I am saying that, in spite
of belief in the pyramid, it can have an effect on
changing experience if used in a certain way.

### How is it used to make wishes come true?

There are several different ways, varying from
ultra-simple to rather complex. The most simple
way is to write what you want on a piece of paper
and stick it under a well-oriented pyramid. If
that's all you do, however, you might as well not
bother. The next important step is reinforcement.
This means to review what you have written every
day and to keep it in mind as frequently as possible. This is done until the wish comes about. It
is important not to change what you have written
unless you have definitely decided you no longer

want it. The more often you change the wish, however, the less effective the process is.

## What's the difference between this and self-suggestion?

The difference is the additional *energy* put into your desire by the pyramid. I will explain this more fully later in the chapter.

## What are some of the more complex ways to use the pyramid for wishes?

Here is a method used by quite a few people. This is more or less the system promoted by Al Manning of E.S.P. Laboratory. A 6-inch pyramid is commonly employed. It can be left plain or each side can be painted or covered with a different color. The colors often chosen are red, blue, green and yellow. When the wish is about an emotional relationship the red side is faced to the north, for healing it is blue, for money it is green, and for intellectual endeavors it is yellow. Similarly colored paper is used for writing the wishes on. Then they are placed inside the pyramid on a platform (often called the "altar" for this type of use) designed to reach up to the one-third point. Manning gives out suggested chants to use as you do this, but some people merely state the wish aloud three times. Every day thereafter, you hold your hands over the north side of the pyramid and repeat the chant or the wish. For a little more complexity, you can leave the paper with the wish on it inside the pyramid for a predetermined time, such as 3, 7, or 9 days. After that you take it out and burn it, using your imagination to sense the wish going out to be fulfilled. The idea behind this is that you have "charged" the wish in the pyramid and now you are releasing it to be accomplished. A few people also take into account the phases of the moon, using the period of the waxing moon to accomplish new things and the waning moon to break up old conditions.

As you can see, there is a powerful lot of suggestion being used in the above method. I call it "window dressing," because it isn't essential to the process itself, although it can be extremely helpful in gaining the cooperation of the subconscious.

Another example of useful window dressing is a pyramid specially constructed for a specific project. A friend of mine makes these for people and takes great pains to do it well. For instance, if a person requests a pyramid for money purposes my friend will transform a simple cardboard pyramid into a "Temple of Prosperity." The pyramid itself will probably be painted green with gold trim, or vice versa. Lines will be drawn on it to give the impression of bricks or blocks and a large dollar sign may be placed on the side to be used for north. The trim will usually be the kind of fancy edging found in sewing shops. Then a base will be made which extends a couple inches out from the bottom of the pyramid. A walkway will be made all around the pyramid and embedded with more dollar signs. From the north side a sumptuous path of some rich-looking material will be leading from the walkway to an elaborately constructed altar in the center, where the person can place his specific wish. After that he follows his own favorite method of reinforcement.

## Can the wish itself be made stronger?

Surely. The wish can be written as if it were already accomplished, such as "I have a new job and am completely happy with it." If you have any artistic talent you can draw yourself in the circumstances you desire and add that to the written wish, or you can obtain a picture or photograph which relates to your wish and include that. A photograph of yourself often helps for reasons that will be gone into below.

## And all this really works?

Within certain limits, yes, it does. Many, many people have used this technique with excellent results. It would be possible to fill a book with case histories, but I'll just give a couple of examples that I wrote up in my research notes.

*Experiment #1*: A friend and I decided to put a wish in the pyramid for a raise in pay at the place where we were working. This was six months before raises were usually given. No mention was made to anyone else about what we were doing or what we wanted. The wish was kept in the pyramid for a week and reinforced every day. At the end of a week it was taken out and destroyed. Two days later the boss announced a raise for the two of us which turned out to be more than we had written on the paper.

*Experiment #2*: The same friend had a problem with his jaw that interfered with his playing a musical instrument. So we placed signed notes under the pyramid directed toward healing his jaw. This was done about 9 a.m. Two days later, at about 3 p.m., the area inside his jaw, which was covered with a layer of tissue and hadn't bothered him when he wasn't playing, "broke open" and began to drain and throb painfully. This was the beginning of a slow healing process.

Naturally, these examples don't prove anything, but they are indicative of what can happen.

*Now will you explain how it happens?*

Okay. The explanation is based on several assumptions and a rather different way of looking at reality that you might not agree with, so feel free to treat what I am going to say as a working hypothesis, even though I will state it as if it were fact.

The assumptions are that telepathy exists, that the life energy with which we have been dealing in this book can be directed by the mind, that a superphysical link exists between objects which have been in proximate contact, and that the life energy can flow along or be transmitted by means of such links, Far out, right?

Here's how it takes place in practice. Whenever you think of something, it goes out to the world as a telepathic broadcast. Other people receive it on a subconscious level, but don't react to it unless it is compatible with their beliefs or is in harmony (or strong disharmony) with their own dominant thoughts. Even then, there may be no reaction if the thought signal is too weak or brief to reach their conscious mind and influence action. Thoughts are powered by life energy, and dominant or sustained thoughts have more energy— therefore more influence—than weak or scattered thoughts. Normally, the only energy people have available for thoughts is the energy surrounding and permeating their own body. This can be considerable when it is concentrated, especially if the body is healthy, but there are ways of accumulating surplus energy from "outside." Yoga, Huna, Zen, Sufism and other systems have specialized techniques often involving breathing, exercise, and visualization for doing this. Another source of extra energy available to all is the pyramid.

The idea of a link between objects is the basis for many psychic practices and what is called "absent healing," which is when one person sends healing energy to another at a distance. Almost always the sender uses a photograph, a signature, or something belonging to the receiver as a means of "tuning in." What I am saying is that there is an actual link between those objects and their owner. It can be thought of as a memory vibration recorded on the object from having been in contact with the owner, in which case the stimulation of the energy field of the object by the addition of extra energy results in a sympathetic reaction by induction on the energy field of the owner. Or, to make it easier to grasp, it can be thought of as an invisible thread along which energy can flow from the object to the person.

Now let's see how these concepts could have operated in the previously mentioned experiments. In Experiment # 1, the subjects wrote their wish on a paper and placed it under the pyramid. A link was established between them and the papers, made stronger by the fact that they wrote on it and included their signatures. The pyramid energy charged the paper and by sympathetic induction this energy was relayed back to the subjects. Every day they spent some time in concentrated thinking about the raise. This thinking went out telepathically to the boss, powered not only by the concentration but by the additional energy the subjects received from the pyramid through their note. The boss must have been receptive to the idea because his subconscious obviously didn't put up any resistance. With the concentration alone, the raise might have come about in a month or two, and without the concentration it would normally have occurred in six months. The extra energy of the pyramid helped the thought penetrate more strongly into the boss's consciousness. I emphasize, however, that if the thought had been strongly opposed to the basic thinking of the boss, the raise would not have been given. He was not in any way forced to do the bidding of the subjects. The process involves persuasion, not command. It is no different than if the subjects had gone in personally to ask for a raise, except that there was no physical confrontation.

In this case there were only the subjects and the boss involved, and so the process could take place easily and quickly. If you should use a wish for a new home, many more people become involved. There is the seller, the broker, the seller's family and friends and yours, the bank personnel, etc. The thought you send out has to affect all of these, and so timing becomes an important factor. You must have patience and persistence.

In Experiment #2 the process was much more simple. Basically, the only thing involved was the adding of extra energy programmed for a specific purpose to the subject with the jaw problem. His own subconscious took care of the rest.

*Couldn't all of this have been coincidence?*

Coincidence can be used to explain anything. So can predestination. Coincidence merely means that things happen by chance. If you believe that everything happens by chance, then there is really no order to the world and it is only an accident that you were born a human being and that you didn't grow up to be an elephant. Yet there is order in the world. An alternative is predestination, which says that a plan for everyone and everything has already been worked out and is fixed. In this case, there is no logical reason why we should try to change the circumstances we find ourselves in. This is a dead-end, initiative-hampering and joy-killing philosophy. Some people will try to combine coincidence, predestination, and causality into an overall view of the world, but the problem with that is there is no way of knowing what is in operation at any given time. The choice is arbitrary.

Thank you very much, but I say that we all create our own experience through our beliefs, thoughts, speech, and actions. In other words, we control our own destiny. The joy of this philosophy is that if we do experience negative conditions, we know we can go on from there and create positive ones. Be free to choose your own view of life, but I'll stick with mine because it works.

*Is it only a theory that there can be a link between objects?*

Not exactly. There have been some objective

demonstrations of this. I spoke with a man working on Kirlian photography experiments at Dr. Thelma Moss's UCLA laboratory who described some experiments using a healer in one room and a subject in another. The subject had his fingers electrophotographed and these were set aside as a control. Then, unknown to the subject, the healer sent energy to the subject while he was being photographed again. Every time out of twelve tries the aura around the subject's fingers increased in size and changed color when the healer sent the energy. The young man with whom I spoke was careful to point out that only twelve runs of a single experiment it proper were involved and so he wasn't allowed to draw any definitive conclusions, but the results do seem to show that energy was being transferred.

In numerous experiments at my own lab we have had subjects write their names on a slip of paper and I have taken them into another room out of their sight. Then, while I repeatedly inserted their signatures into a pyramid and removed it, they would report their sensations to a third party. The insertion of the signature invariably corresponded to visual or sensory impressions felt by the subjects, which would greatly diminish or disappear when the signature was removed. Radionic measurements were also taken, which showed an increase in size of the bioenergy field when the signatures were in the pyramid.

## TROUBLESHOOTING

The most important thing about placing a wish under a pyramid is to make sure it is reasonable enough for your subconscious to accept. If your subconscious doesn't believe that what you have asked for is possible, then the energy will be wasted. While you are consciously sending out a thought for a million dollars, your subconscious will cancel the effect by sending out the thought that you don't really believe you can get it (or that you don't really deserve it, etc.). As with purely physical experiments, the pyramid works best when used to stimulate natural processes.

Don't put too many wishes into the pyramid at the same time. This will scatter the energy and possibly confuse the subconscious. As long as the wishes are not contradictory to each other, your best bet is a separate pyramid for each wish, if you must have several at the same time.

Keep your wish limited to the goal you have in mind. In other words, don't limit yourself by defining the means by which the goal will be accomplished. Just be open to opportunities as they arise.

Maintain as best you can a positive attitude toward the accomplishment of your goal. The more you dwell on doubts, the more you interfere with and slow down the process.

Give careful thought to your goal and its consequences before you put it in the pyramid. Remember the story of King Midas, who got what he wished for—to his regret. Are you prepared to accept the responsibilities that might come with the goal if it is achieved? And do be careful how you word it. The subconscious takes things very literally.

Don't be tempted to use this to harm or exploit anyone. Remember that the programmed energy has to go through you to operate, and you will be the one to be harmed.

I hope this tool will help you create a productive and fulfilling life.

# Chapter 10

# HOW TO BUILD
# YOUR OWN PYRAMID

Now you are going to learn how easy it is to build your own pyramid, even if you don't consider yourself handy with anything. We will cover very simplified methods, move on to more complimated stuff, and give you easy and accurate formulas in terms you can understand. Most of the chapter will deal with Cheops-style pyramids, but we will also describe how to make pyramids of other dimensions.

First we'll start with what might be called the "Classic Research Model." This is a pyramid 6 inches high. It is a handy size for many experiments because it doesn't take up much table space, fits well as a meditation cap, and the focal point is conveniently located at about 2 inches up from the base (for those of you who like precision, I'll give you an exact formula for locating this point before the end of the chapter).

Before going on, in order to set a lot of minds at ease, I wish to make an important announcement. The dimensions of the pyramid are *not*, I repeat, NOT critical. The measurements do *not* have to be exact to the millimeter for it to work. In fact, precision doesn't add anything to the energy generation, within reasonable limits. Your structure should at least look like a pyramid, in other words. But save yourself the hassle of worrying about how accurate your work is. Anyone who tells you the pyramid *must* be precise is spouting comfortable theory, not research results. Precision will have its place in advanced scientific applications, but you should know that the models you make from my directions will be more precise than the Great Pyramid of Gizeh, which doesn't even have base measurements of the same length.

Back to construction. To make the following model you'll need posterboard, a pencil, a ruler, preferably with a metal edge, and a sharp blade. An X-acto knife is good or you can use a gadget that holds razor blades. Even heavy scissors will do. What you are going to do is cut out 4 triangles and tape them together to form a pyramid (so you'll need tape, too).

There are two ways to proceed at this point, the long way and the short way. First the long way: Take your trusty pencil and ruler and draw a line 9⅜ inches long. Mark off the middle of this line, which is at 4 11/16. Now draw a line upwards at right angles to the first line (a protractor will help if you need it, or you can use a book cover by laying the bottom edge along the first line and

using the outer edge of the cover as a guide for
drawing the second line). Make the second line
at least 8 inches long. Next, measure a line from
one end of your first line at an angle so that it
meets the upright line at 8⅝ inches. Do the same
from the other end of the first line (See Fig. 8).

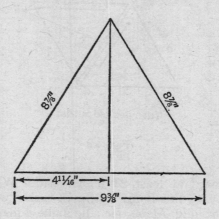

**Figure 8**

Make 4 of these triangles and cut them out. Lay
them down on a table with the shorter sides
touching. There will be a gap between the first
and last triangle (See Fig. 9). Put a strip of tape
along the three joints so that the edges are held
together. Raise the structure up with the tape
on the inside and fold it around. Now tape the
last two triangles together and you have your
Cheops model 6-inch-high pyramid! Easy, wasn't
it?

The shorter way is even easier, but you'll need

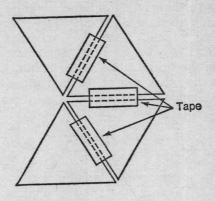

Triangles laid out flat

Figure 9

posterboard at least 24 inches wide. What you do first with this is cut a strip 7½ inches wide and 24 inches long. Along one side make a mark every 9% inches. You'll get two marks. Call this the bottom side. From the top side of the same end you started with, measure out and mark at 4 11/16 inches. Using your straight-edge and your cutting tool, cut through the posterboard from the bottom left-hand corner to the 4 11/16 mark at the top, and then from that point to the first 9%-inch mark. That will give you your first triangle with sides that are automatically the right length. For your second triangle all you have to do is measure out 9% inches from the top left-hand edge and cut from that mark down to the bottom left-hand edge. For the third triangle, make a cut from what is now the top left-hand edge down to the second 9%-inch mark on the bottom, and for the last triangle, repeat the same procedure as for triangle two. Now you have 4 properly proportioned triangles to make your 6-inch-high Cheops pyramid. (See Fig. 10.)

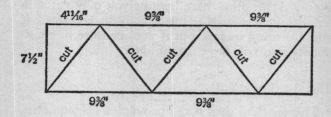

Figure 10

The above method is also ideal for cutting out triangles from styrene or acrylic plastic sheets. From a 2-foot-by-4-foot panel you can get 6 pyramids with a 3-inch strip left over for making platforms. There are inexpensive cutting tools for this that you can get from your dealer. Model airplane glue will hold the triangles together. Sheets that are ⅛-inch thick make good pyramids.

## The Percentage Method

So maybe you are not so much concerned with the height of your pyramid as you are the length of the base. Let's say you have an area into which you would like to fit a pyramid with a 20-inch base length. How do you calculate the length of the sides of each triangular face? Well, it so happens that in Cheops proportions the length of the sides equals the length of the base minus 5 percent. Twenty inches minus 5 percent is exactly 19 inches (20×.05=1; 20−1=19). Therefore you would cut out your triangles with a 20-inch base and two sides of 19 inches each, using the technique described in the first method above. Of course, this particular dimension comes out evenly. With other base lengths you may get side lengths in decimals. This is a little awkward if you are using inches, but if you measure in centimeters you will have no problem.

## The 3-4-5 Method

This method uses some principles of geometry, but it isn't hard. It is based on a triangle in which the base is 3 inches long, a perpendicular at right angles to the base is 4 inches, and the hypotenuse is 5 inches. Applied to a Cheops-style pyramid, the height would be 4 inches, half a base length would be 3 inches, and the distance from the middle of one base side up the face to the tip would be 5 inches. (See Fig 11.) To construct the triangles

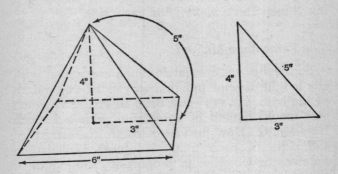

Figure 11

for this pyramid, draw a line 6 inches long and then bisect it with a perpendicular line 5 inches long. Then draw the sides of the triangle from each end of the 6-inch line to the upper end of the 5-inch line. Actually, as you can see, it is very similar to the first method described. Only the dimensions are different. For larger pyramids all you have to do is multiply the dimensions used. For example, a 12-inch base will give you a pyramid 8 inches high, and the height of such a pyramid with a 24-inch base would be 16 inches.

## The 7/11 Method

As I mentioned in my book, *Mana Physics*, this method has no particular advantage other than the mystical connotations of the numbers involved. The ratio is 7 inches of pyramid height for every 11 inches of base length. To measure, draw an 11-inch line and bisect it with a perpendicular line 8⅞ inches long. Draw the sides of your triangle from each end of the 11-inch line to the top of the perpendicular and proceed as in the first method. Some people claim that there are several focal points within the pyramid that correspond to the occult idea of psychic centers, or chakras. In this model, these centers are supposedly at 1-inch intervals from the center of the base to the tip. It would be easier to experiment with this idea if the dimensions were in feet instead of inches. In case you're interested, with an 11-foot base the perpendicular line would be 8 feet, 9⅞ inches.

## The Phi Method

This is my own discovery and will give the most exact results without the necessity for computer calculations. If you are a perfectionist, this is for you. However, for real accuracy you will have to use metric measurements because the dimensions will come out to several decimal places. Pick any base size and divide it in half. Then all you do is multiply that result by 1.618 and the new figure gives you the height for each triangular panel. Let's say, for whatever reasons of your own, that you want a pyramid with a 36-inch base. First you draw that line, and mark the halfway point at 18 inches. Then you make your calculation (18 × 1.618 = 29.124), draw your perpendicular 29.124 inches long and connect the top of that line to the ends of the 36-inch line. Four panels like that, and you've got it made.

All the above methods can be used for making panels of cardboard, plywood, plastic, sheet metal, or any solid panel material. The next method, however, is designed for making a one-piece pyramid out of posterboard, although it can be adapted to thin metals such as tooling copper.

## The One-Piece Pyramid

In addition to the other tools you've already gathered, get yourself a compass—the kind used to draw circles—or a nail, piece of string, and a pencil. What you are going to do first is draw a circle whose radius is the length of one of the corners of your pyramid. That means you have to choose a piece of posterboard large enough to contain the circle you're going to draw.

To make the explanation easier, let's imagine you are going to make a "classic" model with a 9⅜-inch base, and that you will use the nail and string because your compass isn't big enough. Tie your string around the nail at one end and around the pencil at the other, measuring with your ruler so that the distance between the point of the nail and the point of the pencil is 8⅜ inches when both are standing upright. Set the nail in the center of the posterboard, which should be at least about 20 inches square, pull the string taut (try not to get string that is too stretchy), keep the pencil vertical, and draw a circle. Now, with your ruler and pencil, draw a line from the nail hole to the edge of the circle. From this point draw a straight line in a clockwise direction so that it touches the edge of the circle exactly 9⅜ inches away. Do the same thing from this second point to a third point, from the third to a fourth, and from the fourth to a fifth. From the fifth point, draw a line back to the nail hole. Then connect the nail hole with lines to points two, three and four. The last step in the drawing part is to outline a flap which will be used for gluing the whole thing together. Measure ¾ inch from the nail hole along the line to the first point, and from there draw a line parallel to the line from the nail hole to point five (See Fig. 12.)

At last it's cut-out time! With your trusty blade, cut through the posterboard along the very first line from the nail hole to point one, and along all the lines between points. When you get to point five, move over to the flap line and cut along it to the first line you drew. You'll have an easier

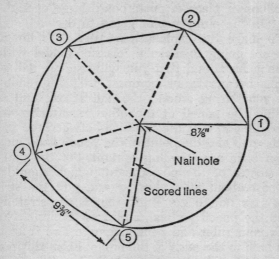

One-piece pyramid

Figure 12

time of it later if you cut away a little section from each end of the flap (shown in the figure as shaded areas). Patience, now, you're almost finished.

The next to the last step is to score (cut only part way through the posterboard) along the lines from the nail hole to points two, three, four and five. Be careful at this stage. You want to score just deeply enough for the posterboard to bend easily. Too light and it will tear away from itself; too deep and you might as well cut out 4 triangles.

The last step is to pick up the fruit of your effort and bend down along all the scored lines to form a perfect pyramid. Spread some white glue along the flap, tuck it under the other free edge, hold it in place with clothespins (you'll find the pyramid will fold flat very nicely for this purpose), wait a half-hour, and voilà! A masterpiece!

Actually, I would recommend keeping your first cut-out without scoring it. That way you can use it for a template or pattern for making future pyramids without going through the hassle of drawing the circle and measuring all the lines. All you'll have to do is outline the pattern, cut, and score.

There are some slight differences if you plan to use this method on something like tooling copper. For one thing, in scoring you will only want to make an indentation in the metal so it can bend. I find that a ballpoint pen is great for this job. For another thing, the sides in the posterboard model have to bend down to form the pyramid, but with metal they will have to bend up. And gluing is trickier, too, because the metal pyramid won't fold flat like the posterboard one. You'll have to spread glue on the flap (white glue seems to work fine), tuck it under the free edge, and lay that side down on a flat surface with something long and heavy inside to weight down the flap.

## Handy Height-Oriented Measurement Chart

It may be that for your purposes the height of the pyramid is all-important and you only need to know the base and corner measurements for the particular height you want. The following chart, in feet and inches, was adapted from one submitted by Capt. N. W. Gambling of California to *The Pyramid Guide* newsletter:

| Height | Base Length | Corner Length |
|--------|-------------|---------------|
| 1 ft. | 1 ft. 6⅞ in. | 1 ft. 5 15/16 in. |
| 2 ft. | 3 ft. 1 11/16 in. | 2 ft. 11⅞ in. |
| 3 ft. | 4 ft. 8 9/16 in. | 4 ft. 5 13/16 in. |
| 4 ft. | 6 ft. 3⅜ in. | 5 ft. 11¾ in. |
| 5 ft. | 7 ft. 10¼ in. | 7 ft. 5 11/16 in. |
| 6 ft. | 9 ft. 5⅛ in. | 8 ft. 11⅝ in. |
| 7 ft. | 11 ft. | 10 ft. 5 9/16 in. |
| 8 ft. | 12 ft. 6 13/16 in. | 11 ft. 11½ in. |

*Framework Pyramids*

All the above methods for figuring out dimensions can be used to calculate the length of the poles, rods, tubes, etc. that you'll need for a framework pyramid. The main concern here is how to connect them together. Of course, you could buy a commercial connector kit, but there are other ways that are lots cheaper.

The cheapest way of all is to use clay. This is good for small models up to about 1 foot in height. The least expensive material for the frame is probably wood doweling, available at hobby shops, lumber yards, or home improvement centers. Pick the diameter of your choice and cut eight pieces according to the dimensions you've chosen—four for the base and four for the corners. When you put it together, remember that the shorter pieces form the corners. Hobby shops also carry small-diameter brass or copper tubes if you prefer that material, or you can get acrylic plastic rods or tubes from a plastic supply house. Anyway, to make the model, all you do is lay out the base pieces and connect them at the corners with a small ball of clay. The corner poles are stuck into the same balls of clay and are held together at the top with another ball of clay. How's that for cheap and simple? And it works.

The "standard" meditation-model framework pyramid is about 4 feet high with a 6-foot base. The easiest way to make this convenient and comfortable size is to cut 4 poles 6 feet long each for the base and four poles each 5 feet 8½ inches long for the corners. I find ¾-inch-diameter poles are the most suitable, whether of wood, copper, or aluminum pipe, PVC plastic pipe, or clear acrylic tubing. Don't get solid plastic rods, because they tend to bend too much.

For connecting the poles I offer you a method that is very inexpensive, yet has many advantages over commercial connectors. The material to use is flexible vinyl tubing, available from a plastic supply house or a good hardware store. Since ¾-inch wood dowel is not really quite ¾ inch in diameter, vinyl tubing with an inside diameter of ¾ inch works fine. It can also be used for the acrylic tubing, but it tends to stick inside the vinyl, so you might want to rub the inside of the vinyl with a little vegetable oil. For the metal and PVC pipe you'll be better off with vinyl tubing with a 1-inch inner diameter.

For each pyramid you'll need 4 feet of vinyl tubing. With heavy scissors or tin snips cut 6 pieces each 6 inches long, and 4 pieces each 3 inches long. Before the next step get 5 bolts about an inch long with nuts. Use your own judgment as to the diameter of the bolts. Just make sure the heads and screws are large enough not to work their way through the vinyl. Also get something pointed like an icepick or an awl. Now you can poke a hole clear through the middle of each 6-inch piece of vinyl and 1 inch from one end of each 3-inch piece. Take 2 of the 6-inch pieces and connect them by shoving a bolt through the holes you made and screwing on the nut. They should be crosswise to each other. This is for the top of your pyramid. Attach each of the 3-inch pieces to the remaining 6-inch pieces in the same way. These are for the bottom corners. For looks, I suggest that the head of the bolt be on the opposite side by the 6-inch vinyl from the 3-inch piece.

To assemble, lay out the base poles on the floor. The two ends of each 6-inch piece of vinyl are for receiving the base poles. The 3-inch piece should be on the inside facing up to receive the corner poles. When the corner poles are in, connect them at the top with the first two 6-inch pieces of vinyl you put together. And there you have it. Apart from the time it took you to purchase the materials, the whole thing ought to take about a half-hour to make. Don't let the rounded top bother you, or the rounded corners. It has virtually no effect on the performance.

One of the biggest advantages of this construction is that it folds up so neatly for transportation, without being taken all apart. Once it is together, merely remove one end of *one* base pole from its vinyl sleeve, and *three* corner poles from their sleeves at the top junction only. Now you will find that all the poles will fold in on each other into a nice, tight, easy-to-carry package. When you are ready to put it up again, lay out the base poles, insert the one base pole into its socket and the three corner ones into theirs at the top, and once again you are ready for pyramidization.

If 6-foot poles are too awkward to carry on your bicycle and you still want to take the pyramid on a picnic, there is another trick you can do with the vinyl. Cut all your poles in half and mark them so you remember which pairs go together, and then cut 8 more 3-inch sections of vinyl. Use these as sleeves to join the cut poles when you put the pyramid back together. Now when you take it down, you only remove the 8 joint sleeves (one end of the sleeve can remain on a pole). The top and bottom halves of the pyramid will fold up into a package not more than 3 feet in length, which can fit into a homemade pack or duffel bag.

Much beyond 8 feet, poles of any kind begin to bend to excess. At that point you have to use something sturdier, like two-by-fours. Since this brings us into the realm of professional carpentry and even engineering, I'm not going to go into it. The purpose of this book is to provide data and directions for amateurs and beginners. Those of you who want to get into large-scale construction can use the methods described previously for your dimensions, but you are on your own for construction details. I will only note that if you are going to build a large enclosed pyramid, be sure to allow for adequate ventilation. Don't bring the sides all the way down to the ground, and install louvres somewhere near the top. It can get mighty stuffy inside a completely enclosed pyramid, even a small one.

*Open-Ended Pyramids*

The only thing different about these pyramids is that one side has been removed or eliminated, leaving three solid side panels and a triangular opening. The purpose is to allow easy access to the interior. "But," you might say, "you can do the same thing with a framework pyramid." That's right, so an open-ended pyramid really becomes useful only when there is a good reason for having side panels. One pyramid modification is to have the side panel opposite the opening made out of mirrored glass or plastic (the other two sides can be plain or mirrored, as you like). This is supposed to have the advantage of reflecting the energy back toward the center. What little work I have done with this type of pyramid does seem to indicate that it increases the intensity of the energy. With this type of pyramid you can also lay a photograph, a striking design, or some colored material on the base and it will be reflected in the mirror. If you have, say, a 6-inch-base pyramid made like this and placed on a shelf that is more or less at eye level you can create a very attractive work of art. And by using various sheets of colored material to lay on the bottom you can change the appearance of your pyramid whenever you like.

Some people are interested in color healing, or the effects of color on plants and other objects. If the three solid panels of the open-ended pyramid are made of translucent colored plastic or glass there are many experiments that can be performed by combining color with pyramid energy.

A third reason for having one open end is to provide easy access and to note visually the progress of experiments with layered pyramids, which I will discuss in the next section.

## Layered Pyramids

There is a rapidly growing interest in the energy work of Wilhelm Reich, a brilliant scientist who died in the late fifties and who was just a little in advance of his time. One of his discoveries was that a layered combination of metallic and organic (or electric and dielectric) materials would accumulate a strong charge of a strange energy that he called "orgone." In some of my early experiments I showed that orgone and pyramid energy are the same thing. This has led to the construction of pyramids with layered side panels and the creation of quite intense fields of energy. The easiest way to make such a pyramid is to use cardboard lined with aluminum foil. Another way is to cut a double set of triangles out of plastic and sandwich triangles of copper within each double panel. Cut the copper a little smaller than the plastic, and glue the plastic together with model airplane glue. Another discovery of Reich was that the more layers you have, the more intense the energy field, but I do not recommend that a beginner try to add more layers without first reading more about Reich's work. I have listed his books in the bibliography.

## Stacked Pyramids

It has been found by various researchers that more energy can be generated if several pyramids are stacked on top of each other with an air space between them. Actually, this is just a modification of Reich's discoveries. Perhaps the simplest way to stack pyramids is to use a needle and thread with cardboard pyramids. As an example, let's use 5 cardboard pyramids with 6-inch bases, and 6 feet of thread. The first step is to tie a button at one end of the thread and run the thread up through the tip of one pyramid with the needle. Tie another button a foot above the first and run the thread through the tip of the next pyramid until it rests on the second button. Keep it up until all 5 pyramids are resting on buttons tied to the thread. This should leave you with about a foot of thread left over with which to tie your stacked set to something overhead. To keep your pyramids in line with each other, tape a connecting thread to one corner of each pyramid. To keep them all in proper alignment, continue this thread up to the overhead and tie (or tape) it there, too. (See Fig. 13.) Your experiment will take place within or under the bottom pyramid.

## Truncated Pyramids

The Great Pyramid of Egypt does not have a capstone. Its top is flat, as are most of the South American pyramids. It has been estimated that about 1 percent of the Great Pyramid's top is missing . . . or was never there in the first place. A lot of legend has grown up about the capstone. Some say it was made of crystal, others say it was made of gold, but no one knows for sure. The possibility that there was never meant to be one has prompted a few of us to experiment with pyramids whose top has been cut off. This gives

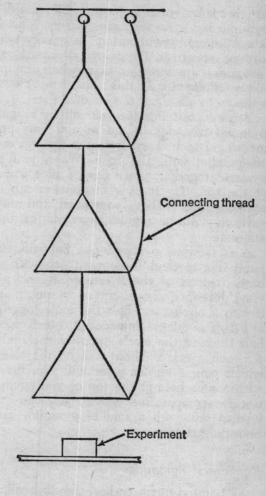

Connecting thread

Experiment

Stacked pyramids

Figure 13

us what is known as a Truncated Pyramid. Such a pyramid has some surprising effects. Most notable is a seeming "downpouring" of energy when you are underneath it. Physiological sensations (body reactions) are stronger than when the pyramid has a regular tip. At this point I don't even have a theory to offer, but the effect is there.

You can test this for yourself by making your pyramid triangles in the regular way and then marking 1 inch down from the tip and cutting it off parallel with the base. When you put the pyramid together, you'll have a nice square hole at the top. Try it as a meditation cap or have someone hold it above your head, and make comparisons with a regular pyramid of the same material.

A framework pyramid can be truncated, too. Here is a method I use with one with a 6-foot base. Instead of the 2 crossed 6-inch pieces of vinyl described above, cut an 18-inch piece, form it into a circle, and bolt the ends together with a 1-inch overlap. Now cut 4 3-inch pieces and bolt them to the circle opposite each other with a 1-inch overlap. These will be the sleeves into which your 4 corner poles will slip, leaving you with a nice hole at the top of your pyramid. To test for comparative effects, you can cover the hole at will with a smaller pyramid. There will be a difference.

## Equilateral Pyramids

As I stated much earlier, the dimensions of the pyramid are not critical for energy effects. You can get the same effects from a pyramid with all sides equal, and they are much easier to make.

Somehow they aren't quite as pleasing to the eye, but they work. Instead of worrying about formulas and relationships of base to sides, all you do is cut the base and sides equal. This is the case whether you use solid panels or frameworks. That's all there is to it.

## Tetrahedrons

A tetrahedron is often described as a pyramid with three sides. The word means four sides, but that includes the base. The important thing is that they, too, work just as well as regular pyramids (some think better). The base and sides of a tetrahedron are equal, making them very easy to construct. The no-hassle way is to make three equal triangles out of posterboard and tape them together. For a framework model, cut 6 poles of equal length and join them with the vinyl corner pieces described before. You won't need the top crosspieces. As a matter of fact, an equilateral framework can easily be transformed into a tetrahedron by removing one base pole and one corner pole and joining the free base ends together. Then you can either leave the top crosspiece as it is or replace it with the extra corner joint.

## Suspending Pyramids

You can use the same technique described in the section on stacked pyramids for suspending a single posterboard pyramid over any area you like, as long as you have a means of attaching it to the ceiling. A tack, nail, or tape will usually do, but sometimes you can't attach anything to the ceiling because of the way it is made. If the ceiling is made of suspended acoustical tiles you can get around this problem by tying the thread or string or wire to a paper clip and bending it to hook over the metal supports. If you want to suspend a lightweight framework pyramid, you can tie the string or whatever to the ends of opposite base poles. Four strings tied to 2 base poles are sufficient. You will need help to keep the pyramid steady and level while you tie it.

When the ceiling doesn't allow for any attachment, then you will have to resort to the wall. One easy way is to simply put up a long plant hanger and suspend your pyramid from that. Suppose you want your pyramid to extend 6 feet out from the wall, though. Here is a method I used over my bed. First I decided how high I wanted the tip of my pyramid to be and drove a nail in the wall at that height (2 nails ½ inch apart would be better). Then I got a 6-foot length of one-by-one. I rested one end on the nail and taped it secure. Next I attached two strings to the other end of the stick and ran them back to the wall where I attached them with nails. These strings were as close to the ceiling as I could get them and about 6 feet apart, with the wall end of the stick between them and lower down. Finally, all I had to do was suspend the pyramid from the outer end of the stick.

For a 6-foot square pyramid "canopy," here is a simple and effective method. I recommend using a plastic framework pyramid because of its light weight. First determine the height that you want your pyramid base to be, given the limitations of your ceiling. Place your base pole in position, make some marks right above and below the pole about a foot from one end, and do the same at the other end. Insert cup hooks or eye bolts at these points, depending on the nature of your wall. Put your base pole between these and tie it in place with string, wire, or whatever. Now tie string or wire to each end of the opposite base pole and run these as near the ceiling as you can along the wall and attach. That'll make you the talk of the neighborhood.

You've got the knowledge. Go out and have fun!

# Chapter 11

# PYRAMID SUPPLIERS

There are those who get a thrill out of doing everything themselves. Some people spend weeks, months or years building boats or cars in their backyards, glorying in the process. Others prefer to have the work already done so they can get on to using the product. For the latter type I am going to list the names and addresses of a number of suppliers of pyramid products and give a brief description of the types of things they carry. This list is by no means all-inclusive. They are only the ones I am most familiar with. I am sure there are many more throughout the country with whom I have not yet made contact. Non-inclusion in this list implies no slight, because I am not necessarily recommending any of the suppliers listed. You'll have to judge the quality of their products for yourself. The list is for information purposes only, as a service to the reader. Most of them are in California, because this is where I live and work. Also, I am only listing those who have products which are uniquely their own (as far as I know).

*Supplier*: Pyramid Power V, Inc.
*Address*:  3015 Nebraska Avenue
            Santa Monica, CA 90404

*Products:* A rather large variety of their own products, many in kit form. They have steel-framework pyramids with 9-inch, 12-inch and 6-foot bases. Also a kit with 3 small 4-inch-base posterboard pyramids and a "Science Lab Kit" which contains a steel-frame pyramid and a number of interesting items for experimentation. In addition, they put out a device for calculating pyramid formulas, pyramid-oriented jewelry, their own books on pyramid energy, and a precision-cast corner kit for which you can supply your own poles to make a meditation pyramid. All their items can be shipped.

*Supplier*: Nick Edwards Environmental
            Systems, Inc.
*Address*:  7650 Haskell Avenue, Suite "D"
            Van Nuys, CA 91406

*Products*: Again, a large variety of their own products, all framework models made from aluminum alloy tubing. The tubing comes in red, orange, blue, or silver. The smaller ones come in a number of sizes and have a plastic platform at the tip to put things on. Their larger models range from 8 feet to 15 feet. Some unique products are overhead-framework matrix systems and a "Pyramid Crystal," which is 2 10-inch framework pyramids connected base to base. They will ship all products.

*Supplier*: Huna Enterprises
*Address*:  2617 Lincoln Blvd.
            Santa Monica, CA 90405

*Products:* This is my own firm. We specialize in products derived from Reich's orgone discoveries, but they also produce 4- and 6-inch-base poster-board pyramids in fluorescent colors, a 12-inch-base plastic framework pyramid that can be made into a tetrahedron, and an unusual device called a "Pyrabloc," which is a pyramid of cast resin containing a copper coil. We also carry books on pyramid energy and products from other suppliers. We make meditation-sized pyramids of wood, plastic, and copper, but these are not shipped.

*Supplier*:  Great Pyramid Cheops
             Research and Development Co.
*Address*:   8143 Big Bend Blvd.
             Webster Grove, MO 63119

*Products*: Aluminum tubular-frame pyramids and grids of various sizes that seem to be direct copies, if not the same, of Nick Edward's systems. They also offer books, jewelry, and energy-related products.

*Supplier*:  Pyramid Products
*Address*:   701 West Ivy
             Glendale, CA 91204

*Products*: Miniature solid pyramid grid systems

$(3'' \times 5''$ or $4'' \times 5'')$ and several sizes of "pyramid energy plates" (zapped rechargeable plates), a pyramid pendulum, foil-lined cardboard pyramids, and several inexpensive pyramid tents (wood frames with plastic covering). Novel item is a "Power Dial," a pyramid with a dial and numbers on one face presumably for use as a wish machine.

*Supplier*: The Pyramid Guide
*Address*: P.O. Box 30305,
　　　　　Santa Barbara, CA 93105

*Products*: Main item is an all-copper-framework pyramid for meditation and sleeping. Also dowsing instruments for detecting pyramid energy, cassettes on pyramid energy, crystals, and a number of books. *The Pyramid Guide* itself is a worthy newsletter for pyramid buffs.

*Supplier*: Electroculture Pyramids
*Address*: 2437 Bayview Avenue,
　　　　　Willowdale, Canada M2L 1A5

*Products*: Five different models in three sizes each of what is called the "Milne Electroculture Pyramid."

*Supplier*: Delta Structures
*Address*: Dept. P.G. 15, Box 2382,
　　　　　Norman, OK 73069

*Products*: Pyramid house plans.

*Supplier*: Edmunds Scientific Company
*Address*: 702 Edscorp Building,
　　　　　Barrington, NJ 08007

*Products*: Edmunds specializes in scientific equipment and experimental items for industry, schools, and hobbyists. Under the heading of "unusual items" they carry a clear acrylic pyramid with a 9¼-inch base which includes a platform, and a slightly smaller cardboard model. They also carry a wide variety of magnets.

From the letters I get, quite a few people are interested in building pyramid homes or cabins, and they request the names of architects or contractors who can draw up specialized plans. Given the required dimensions, I assume that any competent architect could draw up suitable plans. I hear that there is a pyramid community in northern Florida, a pyramid church in Phoenix, and a number of homes in California, as well as plans for building huge pyramid complexes in Neveda and Cairo. However, the only address I have of architects engaged in the design of pyramid homes is California Architects, 9328 Santa Monica Blvd., Beverly Hills, CA.

This list, as I have said, is short and incomplete. A few years from now, someone will probably put out a full directory on sources of pyramid-related products. For a while, all of this will seem like a fad, but it has the makings of a movement. I sincerely hope you will become a part of it.

# ANNOTATED

# BIBLIOGRAPHY

By the time this book goes to press there will probably be more books available on pyramid energy than those listed here. However, at the moment these are the main ones in this very sparse field. I have concentrated, with few exceptions, on books that deal with pyramid energy, and not just with the study of pyramids. Since most articles so far on pyramid energy are either full of tongue-in-cheek skepticism or excerpts from books, I have not bothered to include them. What follows are sources that I have studied, accompanied by my personal comments about them. They are listed in order of copyright date so as to give you some idea of the chronological development of interest. Some of the writings within the works date back to the fifties. It is my preference to list the source by title, rather than author.

*The Cameron Aurameter*, compiled and edited by Meade Layne. Borderland Sciences Research Foundation, Vista, CA; 1972. Mostly about dowsing and the detection of body energy fields with Verne Cameron's special device, the "aurameter," but contains reports of Cameron's early work with pyramids, cones, and magnets.

*Psychic Discoveries Behind the Iron Curtain*, by Sheila Ostrander and Lynn Schroeder. Bantam Books, New York; 1970 (published by Bantam in 1971). This book can be said to have started the real wave of pyramid energy interest in the U.S. As the title implies, it is primarily about psychic research. Chapter 27 is about Drbal's pyramid research, emphasizing the sharpening of razor blades. Also worthwhile from the energy point of view is the next chapter on psychotronic generators.

*Secrets of the Great Pyramid*, by Peter Tompkins. Harper & Row, New York; 1971. Contains only a sentence or so about pyramid energy. The book is mainly valuable for historical, architectural, and mathematical purposes. The best source of general information on the pyramid, in my opinion. The mathematics helped me develop my "phi point" theory.

*The Pyramid and Its Relationship to Biocosmic Energy*, by G. Patrick Flanagan. Self-published, Glendale, CA; 1972. Actually more of a pamphlet than a book, it is the first U.S.-published work dealing just with pyramid energy that I know of. Lists some of his experiments and mathematical data, and includes a small cardboard pyramid.

*Orgone, Reich & Eros*, by W. Edward Mann. Touchstone Books, New York; 1973. Reich's own works (available from Noonday Press or Farrar,

Straus & Giroux) are pretty heavy for the average layman, so I recommend Mann's work as a starter. Unlike many other books about Reich, it stresses the energy experiments, makes correlations with other types of energy, and includes a chapter on Mann's experiments with orgone blankets.

*Pyramid Power*, by Max Toth and Greg Nielsen. Freeway Press, New York; 1974 (recently republished in an expanded and updated version by Warner Books). Part I is a good survey of other pyramids around the world. Part II contains an excellent chapter by Karl Drbal himself.

*Pyramid Power*, by G. Patrick Flanagan. De Vorss & Co., Santa Monica, CA; 1975. One can only assume that Flanagan hadn't read the above book before he titled his. There is some attempt at correlating pyramid energy with other energies, and there is interesting material on Flanagan's own work. Unfortunately, the "ventilated prose" makes for awkward reading, and over a third of the book is devoted to a theory which is extremely difficult to understand and seems to have little to do with pyramid energy.

*The Guide to Pyramid Energy*, by Bill Kerrell and Kathy Goggin. Pyramid Power V, Santa Monica, CA; 1975. One of the better books on pyramid energy, with plenty of thought-provoking experimental data.

*Mana Physics*, by Serge V. King. Huna Enterprises, Los Angeles; 1975. Correlation is the theme of this book, which attempts to prove the relationship between such things as prana, mana, od, orgone, pyramid energy, psychotronic energy, and radionics. Contains information on original experiments in each area.

*The Secret Power of Pyramids*, by Bill Schul

and Ed Pettit. Fawcett Books, New York; 1975. Has a lot of original material and draws from a broad range of scientific and occult sources to back up the claims of pyramid energy effects. A good reference book.

*The Secret Forces of the Pyramids,* by Warren Smith. Zebra Books, New York; 1975. Mostly a historical work about pyramids, with only a slim chapter on the pyramid energy work of others. Emphasis on the occult and mystical aspects of the pyramid.

*Beyond Pyramid Power,* by G. Patrick Flanagan. De Vorss & Co., Marina del Rey, CA; 1975. Some parts are hard to understand for the novice, but it contains some intriguing information on pyramids, cones, and other shapes which produce the same energy.

*The Pyramid Guide,* an international bi-monthly newsletter. El Cariso Publications, Santa Barbara, CA. The only existing open forum for pyramid buffs. Combines scientific and mystical aspects. A must.

On magnetism . . .

*Magnetism and Its Effects on the Living System,* by Albert Roy Davis and Walter C. Rawls, Jr. Exposition Press, New York; 1974.

*The Magnetic Effect,* by the same authors. Exposition Press, New York; 1975. Both the above books deal with extensive studies on treating plants, animals, and humans with magnets. Full of original and remarkable findings that may shed new light on pyramid effects.

# About The Author

SERGE V. KING, Ph.D., has been actively engaged in the fields of parapsychology, paraphysics, bioenergetics, and social technology for more than twenty years. His studies have taken him to many parts of the world, including most of North and South America, Europe, and Africa. During seven years in West Africa he conducted an in-depth study of the magico-religious systems, while at the same time carrying out broad programs of socio-economic development for a private agency. For his latter work he received a medal from the President of Senegal.

Dr. King's work with pyramid energy was an outgrowth of research into ancient and modern claims of forces outside the range of ordinary physics. Not content with evaluating the writings of others, he organized a research group and set up carefully controlled experiments of his own, some of which took as long as three years to complete. Because of his unusual background, he was able to make many correlations and discoveries of his own. Among these was the demonstrable fact that orgone energy and pyramid energy are the same. His practical nature also led him to invent more than a dozen psychoenergetic and bioenergetic devices, some of which have been made available to the public.

The academic qualifications of Dr. King include undergraduate degrees in Asian Studies and Foreign Trade, a master's degree in International Management, and a doctorate in Divinity. The study and use of eight languages has helped to advance his research. An ex-Marine, he is also a member of Phi Beta Kappa.

Initiated by his father into an esoteric order of kahunas at the age of fourteen, Dr. King studied under some of the finest masters of psycho-spiritual knowledge, from Africa to Hawaii. In 1973, with their encouragement, he founded the Order of Huna International, a religious and scientific order dedicated to making known the unknown. Members of the Order engage in bioenergetic and parapsychological research, teaching, counseling, and healing.

In addition to the present book, Dr. King has written *Mana Psysics: A Study of Paraphysical Energy, The Technology of Magic, The Hidden Knowledge of Huna Science, Sexuality and the Zodiac,* and many articles, courses, and lectures in all his fields of endeavor.

At present, Dr. King is teaching, lecturing, writing, researching, heading a corporation, and directing the activities of the Order of Huna International. In addition, he has developed a unique system for achieving inner freedom called Kalana, which is based on his kahuna training and modern bioenergetic research.

Dr. King lives in Malibu, California, with his wife and three children.